W9-CTC-670

College Reading Skills

Topics for the Restless, Book One
Stimulating Selections for Indifferent Readers

Second Edition

Edward Spargo, Editor

WITHDRAWN

Books in the Series:
Book One   Book Three
Book Two   Book Four

Jamestown Publishers
Providence, Rhode Island

Topics for the Restless, Book One

Second Edition

Catalog No. 831
Copyright © 1989 by Jamestown Publishers, Inc.

Cover and text design by Deborah Hulsey Christie

Cover credit: Alexander Calder. *Splotchy.* (1949) Silkscreen on paper. 31 × 55¾ inches. Museum of Art, Rhode Island School of Design; Abby Rockefeller Mauzé Fund

Inside Front Cover: UPI/BETTMAN NEWSPHOTOS
2 The Science of Being Santa: EKM/Nepenthe
3 The Cow-Tail Switch: Woodcut by Mari SanGiovanni
4 The Grand Canyon by Chopper: Copyright 1984 Doug Martin/The Stock Solution
5 Letter Found in a Cement Barrel: Illustration © 1988 Mark Holmes
6 How We Kept Mother's Day: AP/WIDE WORLD PHOTOS
7 Coming of Age on City Streets: Photo courtesy of Covenant House
8 Jonathan Livingston Seagull: © Carl Purcell
9 Will the Weather Channel Save America?: Illustration by Rich Bishop
10 Henrietta, an Intelligent Fish: © Rubin Klass
11 A Whole Society of Loners and Dreamers: Gary Milburn/TOM STACK & ASSOCIATES
12 A Transcendent Moment: Illustration © 1988 Mark Holmes
13 Warm River, I: UPI/BETTMANN NEWSPHOTOS
14 Warm River, II: Woodcut by Mari SanGiovanni
15 Organ Hunter: Ken Shung/© 1988 DISCOVER PUBLICATIONS, INC.
16 Why Not Bicycle to Work?: Wayne Floyd/UNICORN STOCK PHOTOS
17 Bat Guano Can Make a Man Come Face-to-Face with His Values: Illustration by Rich Bishop
18 Children of the A-Bomb: National Archives
19 Alive, I: David & Linda Phillips
20 Alive, II: J. P. Laffont/SYGMA

Printed in the United States
3 4 5 6 7 HS 96 95 94 93 92

ISBN: 0-89061-527-6

Readability			
Book One	F–G	Book Three	J–K
Book Two	H–I	Book Four	L–up

Acknowledgments

Acknowledgment is gratefully made to the following publishers and authors for permission to reprint these selections.

The Science of Being Santa by Roger Rapoport. Copyright © 1973 by Saturday Review Co. First appeared in *Saturday Review/Science* January 1973.

The Cow-Tail Switch. From *The Cow-Tail Switch and Other West African Stories* by Harold Corlander and George Herzog. Copyright © 1962 by Holt, Rinehart & Winston, Inc. Reprinted with permission of Holt, Rinehart & Winston, Inc.

The Grand Canyon by Chopper. Copyright © 1973 by Saturday Review Co. First appeared in *Saturday Review/Society* April 1973.

Letter Found in a Cement Barrel by Hayama Yoshiki. From *Modern Japanese Stories* edited by Ivan Morris. Copyright © 1961. Reprinted with permission of C. E. Tuttle Co., Inc.

How We Kept Mother's Day. Reprinted by permission of Dodd, Mead & Company, Inc. from *Laugh with Leacock* by Stephen Leacock. Copyright © 1930 by Dodd, Mead & Company, Inc. Copyright renewed 1958 by George Leacock.

Coming of Age on City Streets by Patricia Hersch. Reprinted with permission from *Psychology Today* magazine. Copyright © 1988 by the American Psychological Association.

Jonathan Livingston Seagull. Reprinted by permission of Macmillan Publishing Company, Inc. From *Jonathan Livingston Seagull* by Richard Bach. Copyright © 1970 by Richard D. Bach.

Will the Weather Channel Save America? by James Gorman. Copyright © 1987 by James Gorman. First published in *Discover* magazine.

Henrietta, an Intelligent Fish by Pauline L. Jensen. Reprinted with permission from *The National Humane Review.* Copyright © 1973 by the American Humane Association.

A Whole Society of Loners and Dreamers by William Allen. Copyright © 1972 by Saturday Review Co. First appeared in *Saturday Review* December 1972.

Contents

1 | **Introductory Selection**

Explains How the Text is Organized and How to Use It to Maximum Advantage

Vocabulary—The five words below are from the story you are about to read. Study the words and their meanings. Then complete the ten sentences that follow, using one of the five words to fill in the blank in each sentence. Mark your answer by writing the letter of the word on the line before the sentence. Check your answers in the Answer Key on page 106.

A. intent: purpose

B. distribution: arrangement; organization

C. consecutively: in order; one after another

D. corresponding: matching

E. efficient: performing a task easily and skillfully

_____ 1. A wide _____ of topics is needed in order to appeal to all readers.

_____ 2. If you read each chapter _____ , you will understand the lessons more easily.

_____ 3. As you work through each selection, you will become more _____ at analyzing written material.

_____ 4. After finishing the book, you will have a good grasp of its _____ .

_____ 5. The skilled reader has learned that each kind of reading matter demands a _____ reading technique.

_____ 6. The exercises cover a wide _____ of reading and study skills.

_____ 7. In order to be an _____ reader, you must sharpen your critical reading skills.

_____ 8. To communicate with their readers is the _____ of all authors.

_____ 9. Answer the vocabulary questions by writing the letter _____ to the correct word.

_____ 10. Answer the questions _____ , and then turn to the answer key to correct your work.

(Before you begin reading this selection, turn to page 8 and record the hours and minutes in the box labeled *Starting Time* at the bottom of the second column. If you are using this text in class and your instructor has made provisions for timing, you need not stop now; read on.)

It was the intent of the editor to find and include writings which show the real world, the world we all have to face daily.

You are using this text for two purposes: (1) to improve your reading skills, and (2) to read articles and selections designed to make you think. Not every selection will be so demanding, however; many articles were chosen just for pure reading pleasure and enjoyment.

These selections span the range of human experience. It was the intent of the editor to find and include writings which show the real world, the world we all have to face daily. On these pages you will read and learn about current problems facing our society: the use of alcohol and other drugs, the struggle of women for recognition and independence, the seemingly unsolvable problem of disposing of garbage and other wastes of industrial production.

Many selections deal with the quality of our environment and possible new life-styles we may be forced to adopt in the future unless we deal now with air and water pollution, population growth, supplying food needs, caring for the homeless and aged with dignity and respect.

However, many selections treat some of the more pleasant concerns of today's older and more mature student. And finally, some selections just make for enjoyable reading.

Do not expect every selection to be equally interesting to you. In such a wide distribution of subject matter there are bound to be stories which will turn you on, but turn others off. Selections which may bore you, and therefore be hard to read and understand, may very well spark the interest of another reader.

A serious student, therefore, will approach each selection in this text with equal enthusiasm and a determination to succeed. This is the kind of attitude to develop toward reading—an attitude which will serve you well for the rest of your life.

The other purpose for using this text, that of reading and study improvement, recognizes reality, too: the reality of today. This text will help you to develop skills and techniques necessary for efficiency in our society.

Included in each selection are two Study Skills exercises. In these, you will learn methods of understanding, critical thinking skills, techniques of comprehension, and many other key ways to improve your reading ability. Both Study Skills exercises are designed to assist you in developing efficient reading techniques. As you read the selections in this book, you will find that often one Study Skills exercise leads directly to the next. It is important to read and work the Study Skills exercises consecutively in order to understand fully each subject.

Today's reader must be flexible enough to choose from a supply of skills one that is suitable for each reading task. The skilled reader has learned that each kind of reading matter demands a corresponding reading technique—there is no single "best" way to read. As you complete the selections and exercises in this book, you will find yourself growing in technique.

Using the Text

The twenty selections are designed to be read in numerical order, starting with the Introductory Selection and ending with Selection 20. Because the selections increase in difficulty as you progress through the book, the earlier ones prepare you to handle successfully the upcoming ones.

Here are the procedures to follow for reading each selection.

1. Answer the Vocabulary Questions. Immediately preceding each selection is a vocabulary previewing exercise. The exercise includes five vocabulary words from the selection, their meanings, and ten fill-in-the-blank sentences. To complete each sentence you will fill in the blank with one of the five vocabulary words.

Previewing the vocabulary in such a fashion will give you a head start on understanding the words when you encounter them in the selection. The fill-in-the-blank sentences present each word in context (surrounding words). That provides you with the chance to improve your ability to use context as an aid in understanding words. The efficient use of context is a valuable vocabulary tool.

After you have filled in the blanks in all ten sentences, check your answers in the Answer Key that starts on page 106. Be sure you understand the correct meaning of any wrong answers.

2. Preview before Reading. Previewing acquaints you with the overall content and structure of the selection before you actually read. It is like consulting a road map before taking a trip: planning the route gives you more confidence as you proceed and, perhaps, helps you avoid any unnecessary delays. Previewing should take about a minute or two and is done in this way:

a) Read the Title. Learn the writer's subject and, possibly, his point of view on it.

b) Read the Opening and Closing Paragraphs. These contain the introductory and concluding remarks. Important information is frequently presented in these key paragraphs.

c) Skim through. Try to discover the author's approach

to his subject. Does he use many examples? Is his purpose to sell you his ideas? What else can you learn now to help you when you read?

3. Read the Selection. Do not try to race through. Read well and carefully enough so that you can answer the comprehension questions that follow.

Keep track of your reading time by noting when you start and finish. A table on page 110 converts your reading time to a words-per-minute rate. Select the time from the table that is closest to your reading time. Record those figures in the boxes at the end of the selection. There is no one ideal reading speed for everything. The efficient reader varies his speed as the selection requires.

Some selections include a brief biography. Do not include this in your reading time. It is there to introduce you to the writer. Many of the selections have been reprinted from full-length books and novels. If you find a particular selection interesting, you may enjoy reading the entire book.

4. Answer the Comprehension Questions. After you have read the selection, find the comprehension questions that follow. These have been included to test your understanding of what you have read. The questions are diagnostic, too. Because the comprehension skill being measured is identified, you can detect your areas of weakness.

Read each question carefully and, without looking back, select one of the four choices given that answers that question most accurately or most completely. Frequently all four choices, or options, given for a question are *correct*, but one is the *best* answer. For this reason the comprehension questions are highly challenging and require you to be highly discriminating. You may, from time to time, disagree with the choice given in the Answer Key. When this happens, you have an opportunity to sharpen your powers of discrimination. Study the question again and seek to discover why the listed answer may be best. When you disagree with the text, you are thinking; when you objectively analyze and recognize your errors, you are learning.

The Answer Key begins on page 106. Find the answers for your selection and correct your comprehension work. When you discover a wrong answer, circle it and check the correct one.

The boxes following each selection contain space for your comprehension and vocabulary scores. Each correct vocabulary item is worth ten points and each correct comprehension answer is worth ten points.

Pages 111 and 112 contain graphs to be used for plotting your scores and tallying your incorrect responses.

On page 111 record your comprehension score at the appropriate intersection of lines, using an *X*. Use a circle, or some other mark, on the same graph to record your vocabulary results. Some students prefer to use different color inks, or pencil and ink, to distinguish between comprehension and vocabulary plottings.

On page 112 darken in the squares to indicate the comprehension questions you have missed. By referring to the Skills Profile as you progress through the text, you and your instructor will be able to tell which questions give you the most trouble. As soon as you detect a specific weakness in comprehension, consult with your instructor to see what supplementary materials he or she can provide or suggest.

A profitable habit for you to acquire is the practice of analyzing the questions you have answered incorrectly. If time permits, return to the selection to find and underline the passages containing the correct answers. This helps you to see what you missed the first time. Some interpretive and generalization type questions are not answered specifically in the text. In these cases bracket that part of the selection that alludes to the correct answer. Your instructor may recommend that you complete this step outside of class as homework.

5. Complete the Study Skills Exercises. Following the comprehension questions in each chapter is a passage on study skills. Some of the sentences in the passage have blanks where words have been omitted. Next to the passage are groups of five words, one group for each blank. Your task is to complete the passage by selecting the correct word for each of the blanks.

Next are five completion questions to be answered after you have reread the study skills passage.

The same answer key you have been using gives the correct responses for these two study skills exercises.

If class time is at a premium, your instructor may prefer that you complete the exercises out of class.

The following selections in this text are structured just like this introductory one. Having completed this selection and its exercises, you will then be prepared to proceed to Selection 2.

Starting Time			*Finishing Time*	
Reading Time			*Reading Rate*	
Comprehension			*Vocabulary*	

Comprehension— Read the following questions and statements. For each one, put an *x* in the box before the option that contains the most complete or accurate answer. Check your answers in the Answer Key on page 106.

1. How much time should you devote to previewing a selection?
   - ☐ a. Your time will vary with each selection.
   - ☐ b. You should devote about one or two minutes to previewing.
   - ☐ c. No specific time is suggested.
   - ☐ d. None—the instructor times the selection.

2. The way that the vocabulary exercises are described suggests that
   - ☐ a. the meaning of a word often depends on how it is used.
   - ☐ b. the final authority for word meaning is the dictionary.
   - ☐ c. words have precise and permanent meanings.
   - ☐ d. certain words are always difficult to understand.

3. The writer of this passage presents the facts in order of
   - ☐ a. importance.   ☐ c. time.
   - ☐ b. purpose.   ☐ d. operation.

4. *Topics for the Restless* is based on which of the following premises?
   - ☐ a. All students are restless.
   - ☐ b. Some students learn best when they are restless.
   - ☐ c. Writings dealing with real problems and situations should interest many students.
   - ☐ d. All of the selections in this text should interest all students.

5. How does the writer feel about reading speed?
   - ☐ a. It is a minimal aspect of the total reading situation.
   - ☐ b. It is second (following comprehension) in the ranking of skills.
   - ☐ c. It is connected to comprehension.
   - ☐ d. It should be developed at an early age.

6. The introductory selection
   - ☐ a. eliminates the need for oral instruction.
   - ☐ b. explains the proper use of the text in detail.
   - ☐ c. permits the student to learn by doing.
   - ☐ d. allows for variety and interest.

7. The introductory selection suggests that
   - ☐ a. most readers are not flexible.
   - ☐ b. students should learn to use different reading skills for different types of reading matter.
   - ☐ c. students today read better than students of the past did.
   - ☐ d. twenty selections is an ideal number for a reading improvement text.

8. The overall tone of this passage is
   - ☐ a. serious.   ☐ c. humorous.
   - ☐ b. suspenseful.   ☐ d. sarcastic.

9. The author of this selection is probably
   - ☐ a. a doctor.   ☐ c. an educator.
   - ☐ b. an accountant.   ☐ d. a businessman.

10. The writer of this passage makes his point clear by
   - ☐ a. telling a story.
   - ☐ b. listing historical facts.
   - ☐ c. using metaphors.
   - ☐ d. giving directions.

Comprehension Skills

1. recalling specific facts	6. making a judgment
2. retaining concepts	7. making an inference
3. organizing facts	8. recognizing tone
4. understanding the main idea	9. understanding characters
5. drawing a conclusion	10. appreciation of literary forms

Study Skills, Part One—Following is a passage with blanks where words have been omitted. Next to the passage are groups of five words, one group for each blank. Complete the passage by selecting the correct word for each of the blanks.

Previewing

Students frequently ask, "What can I do to improve my reading?" Believe it or not, there is a one-word answer to that __(1)__ : preview.

The single most __(2)__ technique that you can acquire in any reading course is the habit of previewing.

(1)   course   question
   statement   theory   lesson

(2)   important   difficult
   statement   divided   natural

Most students jump in with the first word and try to meet the author's ideas head-on. That is a poor ___(3)___ because it is inefficient.

Athletic coaches, for example, scout their opponents before upcoming games to see how they play. That allows them to form a game ___(4)___ for their team to follow.

To be efficient in reading, you must do the same thing—scout the author to see how he writes. That will help you discover the best way to read the work.

What do you do before assembling a jigsaw puzzle? You probably study the picture to see what the puzzle looks like with the pieces in the proper ___(5)___ .

Do that in reading as well. See the whole picture before you begin putting the words and ideas together. See where the author is going, what he plans to say, and what concepts or examples he uses to present his ideas. If you can discover the author's main point and the arguments ___(6)___ it, you can begin to organize and interpret the ideas right away; hence, you can read intelligently and see how everything fits.

Don't read at a disadvantage. Preview first to get the whole picture. There are no educational guarantees in life, but this is as close as you can come to ensuring better reading and comprehension in less time.

Pregame warmups (to cite another athletic example) improve player performance on the ___(7)___ . Likewise, previewing can improve your performance on the page.

(3) invention   approach
     relationship   value   advantage

(4)   plan   supply
     appearance   overhead   bond

(5)   sources   measures
     places   quantities   perspectives

(6)   supposing   placing
     presenting   discovering   supporting

(7)   whole   field
     rules   trail   water

Study Skills, Part Two—Read the study skills passage again, paying special attention to the lesson being taught. Then, without looking back at the passage, complete each sentence below by writing in the missing word or words. Check the Answer Key on page 106 for the answers to Study Skills, Part One, and Study Skills, Part Two.

1. _____ to improve your performance on the page.

2. Athletic coaches _____ their opponents to see how they play.

3. You should see the whole _____ before you begin putting the words and ideas together.

4. You should look for the concepts or _____ the author uses to present ideas.

5. You can begin to _____ and interpret the author's ideas right from the start.

2 | **The Science of Being Santa**

by Roger Rapoport

Vocabulary—The five words below are from the story you are about to read. Study the words and their meanings. Then complete the ten sentences that follow, using one of the five words to fill in the blank in each sentence. Mark your answer by writing the letter of the word on the line before the sentence. Check your answers in the Answer Key on page 106.

A. comprehensive: broad in scope

B. essential: necessary; indispensable

C. hygiene: cleanliness

D. compliance: agreement with or positive action for something

E. resumed: started again

_____ 1. Western Girl considers it _____ that Santas not be seen smoking.

_____ 2. It is important that Santas not neglect personal _____ .

_____ 3. A Santa with body odor was fired by Western Girl after his _____ problem was discovered.

_____ 4. _____ with company rules is expected of all Western Girl Santas.

_____ 5. Most department stores consider Santa an _____ part of their holiday promotions.

_____ 6. After Christmas, most Western Girl Santas presumably _____ other activities.

_____ 7. Western Girl offers a _____ training program to its Santas.

_____ 8. After a break for coffee and doughnuts, Mrs. Plowe _____ teaching.

_____ 9. Western Girl can be proud of its _____ with equal opportunity laws.

_____ 10. Western Girl offers stores a _____ package, including fully bonded Santas and backups in case of emergency.

At Santa School, it's not "on Dasher, on Dancer," but "on Dial, on Certs, and on Brylcreem."

Mrs. Gail Plowe slapped her hand on a red velveteen suit trimmed with white fur as she addressed her students: "Now, class, under no circumstances does Western Girl tolerate 'Ho, Ho, Ho'-ing from our Santas. You'll frighten the smaller children right out of the store. Try to remember you're in there as a customer draw. A Santa can make or break a store at Christmastime."

Mrs. Plowe's twenty-two Santa trainees shifted uneasily in their chairs at the Oakland, California, office of Western Girl, the international temporary-employment agency. They ranged from eighteen to seventy, from the unemployed to the retired. But primarily they were hirsute young college students eager to make a few hundred extra dollars by playing St. Nicholas. Theirs was one of seventy-five pre-Christmas Santa schools conducted across the country by Western Girl's Santa Division. With a full-time Santa selling for $1,200 to $1,500, the company expects to gross roughly $500,000 on the rental of 500 full- and part-time Santas this season.

Western Girl has become the nation's largest supplier of Santas, thanks in large part to a comprehensive training program pioneered by Richard Westerman of the North Pole Santa Claus Rental Agency in Los Angeles. Three years ago Western Girl bought out the North Pole Agency and took Westerman's total-service-Santa concept national. Today a store anywhere in the country can rent a fully trained and costumed Western Girl Santa, "bonded to $100,000 and covered with $1 million worth of insurance for bodily injury and property damage." In case of illness a backup Santa is available. This approach has yielded an average annual sales gain of 30 percent, as such department-store chains as Sears, Ward's, and Penney's rent more and more Western Girl Santas each year in order to free themselves from the headaches of the Santa business.

The temporary employment agency screens carefully; only one out of every twenty-three Santa applicants is selected. A week before Thanksgiving, matronly Mrs. Plowe stressed this point to her Oakland students: "Age and weight have very little to do with your being here tonight. When you get dressed up in the suit, about all anyone can see is your eyes. All of you have been chosen primarily because of that essential twinkle in your eyes." Her students blushed and winked at each other.

Mrs. Plowe glanced down at her thick, red Santa manual and continued lecturing: "There are several ground rules you must observe to stay in the Santa corps. I don't want to catch any of you with a bright red nose brought on from nipping at a bottle of Old Grandad. You're not allowed to flirt with the young women who work as Santa's helpers. Please remove your beard before you light a cigarette, or it might catch fire. Don't let the kids catch you smoking.

"If you're not working, don't let the kids see you in a Santa suit. Don't be like the off-duty Santa who brushed a friendly child aside, grumbling, 'Go away, little girl; I'm not on until the afternoon shift.' When you change shifts with another Santa, make sure you are back in the dressing room before your replacement shows up in front of the children—it confuses the kids when they see two Santas at the same time. And please, please, pay attention to personal hygiene. We had to send one Santa home last year because of b. o. So remember, it's: 'On Right Guard, on Dial, on Certs, on Pepsodent, on Listerine, and on Brylcreem.'

"Now the most important thing you have to learn before you go to work is the names of the reindeer . . . Dasher, Dancer, Prancer, Vixen, Comet, Cupid, Donner, and Blitzen."

One bearded student wearing a work shirt and jeans raised his hand and asked: "What about Rudolph?"

Mrs. Plowe nodded: "Yes, of course, Rudolph. And let's all remember that Rudolph has a girlfriend named Violet."

Consulting her manual once again, the instructor began teaching Santa patter guaranteed to engage even the toughest kid: "The three basic parts of our Santa talk are the invitation, recognition of the child, and questions-closing. To save time that would normally be devoted to finding out the child's name, simply invite each 'young man' or 'young woman' to sit down with you. Next, recognize how they've grown since last year: 'Young man, you've sprouted up like a weed,' or, 'You're even prettier than last year, young woman.' Then ask what they want for Christmas and close by telling them to behave, eat their vegetables, drink their milk, and brush their teeth twice daily. Adjust your speed to the number of youngsters standing in line. Under pressure, speed up your pitch in order to get more youngsters through faster.

"Never promise anything. Always say you'll see what you can do. If they ask for a baby brother, tell them: 'That's out of my department. If you want a baby brother, you should pray for one. If God wants you to have one, then you will get one.' Never mention the word 'parents.' Use the term 'folks,' because a large percentage of kids today are not living with their original mothers and fathers. Many are in foster homes, or with grandparents or other relatives. If you say 'parents,' they might break out sobbing, 'I haven't any daddy or mommy,' and become semihysterical."

When Mrs. Plowe had finished teaching the Santa patter, her class broke for coffee and doughnuts. Much of their conversation was about the $500 to $700 that each expected to make during the Yuletide season. Although wages would be minimal, everyone was confident about regular overtime opportunities. The students seemed delighted that Western Girl was paying them to attend Santa school.

Gradually the pupils clustered around four classmates with previous Santa experience. Skip Ball, a nineteen-year-old student at nearby Diablo Valley College, encouraged the new Santas to limit themselves to four-hour shifts when possible: "Going eight hours is a real strain, with all these kids tugging at your beard and asking for weird things like pet rats. Last year I worked in a Walnut Creek department store where one of the Santas freaked out. He started running through the toy department, giving things away. The guy thought he really was Santa Claus. They had to fire him."

Another Santa returnee, who works as a handyman during the off-season, warned everyone to beware of adults: "Last year I worked at Penney's, and a lot of grownups sat down on my lap and told me what they wanted for Christmas. One woman must have weighed 250 pounds."

Marvin Meyers, a husky twenty-year-old black singer with an Oakland band, alerted the students to special problems brought on by Western Girl's steadfast compliance with all the federal equal-employment-opportunity regulations. "I worked at Ward's here in Oakland last Christmas and split the day with a white Santa. One little kid showed up twice in a single day and became really confused. He gave me a long look and asked: 'Santa, what's happened to your face?' I told him I'd just been out here in the California sun too long." Another student mentioned that he had heard about similar problems caused by Western Girl's occasional use of women Santas. Curious children have asked Santa why he suddenly had sprouted breasts.

James McMahan, another twenty-year-old black from Oakland, mentioned that once he had played Santa to a child who happened to glance out the store window and noticed another Santa riding on top of a parade bus: "I told the kid that was Santa and I was St. Nick. He believed me. Generally, though, I think you'll find the younger generation different from our own. They really know what they want."

When class had resumed, Mrs. Plowe held up a pair of Santa pants and showed how a drawstring makes one size fit all. Next, she pointed out a special secret pocket: "This was invented several years ago after eleven Santas had their wallets stolen out of dressing rooms. We encourage you to use it for your valuables."

Then, with the help of Bruce Leiper, a tall twenty-two-year-old Berkeley student, she showed everyone how to put on the pants, jacket, belt, spats, eyeshadow, wig, and beard. At this point the class was officially over, but Mrs. Plowe simply couldn't resist the temptation offered by her two black students: "You black guys look so adorable as Santas. Would one of you consider dressing up?"

Marvin Meyers and James McMahan flipped a nickel, and McMahan lost. He suited up quickly, to the cheers of his classmates. A moment later Western Girl's Oakland office cleaning lady showed up with her young daughter. McMahan promptly bounced the child onto his knee and asked, "What do you want for Christmas, young lady?"

The little girl stared out at the classroom full of future Santas but refused to utter a word.

Starting Time			Finishing Time	
Reading Time			Reading Rate	
Comprehension			Vocabulary	

Comprehension

Comprehension — Read the following questions and statements. For each one, put an *x* in the box before the option that contains the most complete or accurate answer. Check your answers in the Answer Key on page 106.

1. Western Girl Santa is an outgrowth of the
   □ a. North Pole Santa Claus Rental Agency.
   □ b. pre-Christmas Santa schools.
   □ c. temporary employment agencies.
   □ d. national unemployment situation.

2. An important qualification for being hired to play Santa is
   □ a. proven maturity.
   □ b. expressive eyes.
   □ c. body size.
   □ d. short stature.

3. People enroll in Santa school
   □ a. in order to apply for a job as Western Girl Santas.
   □ b. after being hired as Western Girl Santas.
   □ c. in order to become freelance Santas.
   □ d. if they have difficulty adjusting to their roles as Santa.

4. The purpose of this article is to
   □ a. recruit Santa candidates.
   □ b. describe an unusual service.
   □ c. revive the spirit of Christmas.
   □ d. promote good relations.

5. Stores who hire Santas from Western Girl
☐ a. cannot train their own Santas.
☐ b. must take out insurance in order to protect themselves.
☐ c. select and train their own candidates.
☐ d. want to attract parents of small children.

6. Department-store Santas must expect to
☐ a. see unpredictable behavior.
☐ b. be recognized.
☐ c. work during the off-season.
☐ d. be fired.

7. Being a department-store Santa can be
☐ a. frightening.   ☐ c. degrading.
☐ b. stressful.   ☐ d. debilitating.

8. The tone of Mrs. Plowe's lecture was
☐ a. matter-of-fact.
☐ b. disheartening.
☐ c. impatient.
☐ d. frivolous.

9. The Santa trainees in this selection were
☐ a. desperate for money.
☐ b. easily embarrassed.
☐ c. willing pupils.
☐ d. recalcitrant pupils.

10. When James McMahan says "I think you'll find the younger generation different from our own," he means the younger generation is
☐ a. more intense than his generation.
☐ b. more socially aware than his generation.
☐ c. wealthier than his generation.
☐ d. more selfish than his generation.

Comprehension Skills

1. recalling specific facts	6. making a judgment
2. retaining concepts	7. making an inference
3. organizing facts	8. recognizing tone
4. understanding the main idea	9. understanding characters
5. drawing a conclusion	10. appreciation of literary forms

Study Skills, Part One—Following is a passage with blanks where words have been omitted. Next to the passage are groups of five words, one group for each blank. Complete the passage by selecting the correct word for each of the blanks.

How to Preview, I

Previewing is known by many names. It is called *surveying* and *prereading* too. The first three steps in previewing are as follows:

1. Read the Title. You would normally do that before reading a selection, but in previewing we want you to be ___(1)___ of what you can *learn* from the title. Not only can you learn the author's subject, you can frequently learn how he or she *feels* about that subject. W. H. Auden once wrote an essay entitled *Poetry Must Praise*. From the title you can discern the author's feeling, and you would expect to read ___(2)___ supporting his position and illustrations demonstrating his case. With just that little bit of ___(3)___ , a reader can approach the selection intelligently, knowing what to expect.

An author named Mark Clifton wrote an article called *The Dread Tomato Addiction*. Judging by the title, you could reasonably expect to find ___(4)___ or satire in the author's account.

Headlines and titles are thought to be quite influential by authors and editors. Indeed, many magazines survive on the appeal or ___(5)___ value of the titles of their articles.

2. Read the Subheads. In textbooks especially, and in many magazines as well, subheads follow the title to give the reader more information on the subject. In textbooks,

(1) | hopeful | aware |
| jealous | indifferent | certain |

(2) | articles | announcements |
| letters | arguments | references |

(3) | information | courage |
| direction | hesitancy | informality |

(4) | imagination | intelligence |
| humility | tragedy | humor |

(5) | sensitive | shock |
| serious | survival | literary |

subheads often take the form of one-line digests of the chapter—"Here's what we are going to cover." In magazines, "teaser" statements follow the title to further spark the reader's ___(6)___ . Look for subheads whenever you are previewing.

3. Read the Illustrations. If a picture or illustration accompanies the article, don't glance at it and move on, *read* it. Interpret it to learn what you can about the ___(7)___ of the article. You have no doubt heard it said that a picture is worth a thousand words. You can prove the worth of that observation by studying the illustrations when previewing. In other words, see what you can learn visually before reading.

(6) currency   urgency
    satisfaction   disgust   interest

(7) flavor   attitude
    content   author   popularity

Study Skills, Part Two—Read the study skills passage again, paying special attention to the lesson being taught. Then, without looking back at the passage, complete each sentence below by writing in the missing word or words. Check the Answer Key on page 106 for the answers to Study Skills, Part One, and Study Skills, Part Two.

1. The first step in previewing is _____ .

2. The first step can tell you not only the author's subject, but also his _____ about the subject.

3. Many magazines survive on the appeal of the _____ of their articles.

4. The subheads in textbooks frequently give a one-line _____ of the chapters.

5. It has been said that a picture is worth a thousand _____ .

3 The Cow-Tail Switch

West African Folktale

Vocabulary—The five words below are from the story you are about to read. Study the words and their meanings. Then complete the ten sentences that follow, using one of the five words to fill in the blank in each sentence. Mark your answer by writing the letter of the word on the line before the sentence. Check your answers in the Answer Key on page 106.

A. grazed: fed on grass and foliage

B. seeped: passed slowly

C. hover: hang suspended; linger

D. detained: delayed

E. clamor: loud outcry

_____ 1. Many cows _____ in the fields around Kundi.

_____ 2. If nothing had _____ him, Ogaloussa's hunt would have lasted only a few hours.

_____ 3. Darkness seemed to _____ over the deep forest.

_____ 4. When Ogaloussa did not return from his hunt, his sons wondered what had _____ him.

_____ 5. When the sons found Ogaloussa in the forest, his blood had long since _____ into the ground.

_____ 6. The animals of Kundi _____ in grassland, not in rice fields or cassava fields.

_____ 7. As the celebration over Ogaloussa's return began, excitement seemed to _____ in the air.

_____ 8. There was quite a _____ over the cow-tail switch.

_____ 9. The _____ of the villagers ceased when Ogaloussa stood up to speak.

_____ 10. Smoke routinely _____ through the roofs of Kundi's clay houses.

Near the edge of the Liberian rain forest, on a hill overlooking the Cavally River, was the village of Kundi. Its rice and cassava fields spread in all directions. Cattle grazed in the grassland near the river. Smoke from the fires in the round clay houses seeped through the palmleaf roofs, and from a distance these faint columns of smoke seemed to hover over the village. Men and boys fished in the river with nets, and women pounded grain in wooden mortars before the houses.

In this village, with his wife and many children, lived a hunter by the name of Ogaloussa.

One morning Ogaloussa took his weapons down from the wall of his house and went into the forest to hunt. His wife and his children went to tend their fields, and drove their cattle out to graze. The day passed, and they ate their evening meal of manioc and fish. Darkness came, but Ogaloussa didn't return.

Another day went by, and still Ogaloussa didn't come back. They talked about it and wondered what could have detained him. A week passed, then a month. Sometimes Ogaloussa's sons mentioned that he hadn't come home. The family cared for the crops, and the sons hunted for game, but after a while they no longer talked about Ogaloussa's disappearance.

Then, one day, another son was born to Ogaloussa's wife. His name was Puli. Puli grew older. He began to sit up and crawl. The time came when Puli began to talk, and the first thing he said was, "Where is my father?"

The other sons looked across the rice fields.

"Yes," one of them said. "Where is Father?"

"He should have returned long ago," another one said.

"Something must have happened. We ought to look for him," a third son said.

"He went into the forest, but where will we find him?" another one asked.

"I saw him go," one of them said. "He went that way, across the river. Let us follow the trail and search for him."

So the sons took their weapons and started out to look for Ogaloussa. When they were deep among the great trees and vines of the forest they lost the trail. They searched in the forest until one of them found the trail again. They followed it until they lost the way once more, and then another son found the trail. It was dark in the forest, and many times they became lost. Each time another son found the way. At last they came to a clearing among the trees, and there on the ground scattered about lay Ogaloussa's bones and his rusted weapons. They knew then that Ogaloussa had been killed in the hunt.

One of the sons stepped forward and said, "I know how to put a dead person's bones together." He gathered all of Ogaloussa's bones and put them together, each in its right place.

"I shall give it to the one who did the most to bring me home."

Another son said, "I have knowledge too. I know how to cover the skeleton with sinews and flesh." He went to work, and he covered Ogaloussa's bones with sinews and flesh.

A third son said, "I have the power to put blood into a body." He went forward and put blood into Ogaloussa's veins, and then he stepped aside.

Another of the sons said, "I can put breath into a body." He did his work, and when he was through they saw Ogaloussa's chest rise and fall.

"I can give the power of movement to a body," another of them said. He put the power of movement into his father's body, and Ogaloussa sat up and opened his eyes.

"I can give him the power of speech," another son said. He gave the body the power of speech, and then he stepped back.

Ogaloussa looked around him. He stood up.

"Where are my weapons?" he asked.

They picked up his rusted weapons from the grass where they lay and gave them to him. They then returned the way they had come, through the forest and the rice fields, until they had arrived once more in the village.

Ogaloussa went into his house. His wife prepared a bath for him and he bathed. She prepared food for him and he ate. Four days he remained in the house, and on the fifth day he came out and shaved his head, because this was what people did when they came back from the land of the dead.

Afterwards he killed a cow for a great feast. He took the cow's tail and braided it. He decorated it with beads and cowry shells and bits of shiny metal. It was a beautiful thing. Ogaloussa carried it with him to important affairs. When there was a dance or an important ceremony he always had it with him. The people of the village thought it was the most beautiful cow-tail switch they had ever seen.

Soon there was a celebration in the village because Ogaloussa had returned from the dead. The people dressed in their best clothes, the musicians brought out their instruments, and a big dance began. The drummers beat their drums and the women sang. The people drank much palm wine. Everyone was happy.

Ogaloussa carried his cow-tail switch, and everyone admired it. Some of the men grew bold and came forward to Ogaloussa and asked for the cow-tail switch, but Ogaloussa kept it in his hand. Now and then there was a clamor and much confusion as many people asked for it at once. The women and children begged for it too, but Ogaloussa refused them all.

Finally he stood up to talk. The dancing stopped and people came close to hear what Ogaloussa had to say.

"A long time ago I went into the forest," Ogaloussa said. "While I was hunting I was killed by a leopard. Then my sons came for me. They brought me back from the land of the dead to my village. I will give this cow-tail switch to one of my sons. All of them have done something to bring me back from the dead, but I have only one cow tail to give. I shall give it to the one who did the most to bring me home."

So an argument started.

"He will give it to me!" one of the sons said. "It was I who did the most, for I found the trail in the forest when it was lost!"

"No, he will give it to me!" another son said. "It was I who put his bones together!"

"It was I who covered his bones with sinews and flesh!" another said. "He will give it to me!"

"It was I who gave him the power of movement!" another son said. "I deserve it most!"

Another son said it was he who should have the switch, because he had put blood in Ogaloussa's veins. Another claimed it because he had put breath in the body. Each of the sons argued his right to possess the wonderful cow-tail switch.

Before long not only the sons but the other people of the village were talking. Some of them argued that the son who had put blood in Ogaloussa's veins should get the switch, others that the one who had given Ogaloussa's breath should get it. Some of them believed that all of the sons had done equal things, and that they should share it. They argued back and forth this way until Ogaloussa asked them to be quiet.

"To this son I will give the cow-tail switch, for I owe most to him," Ogaloussa said.

He came forward and bent low and handed it to Puli, the little boy who had been born while Ogaloussa was in the forest.

The people of the village remembered then that the child's first words had been, "Where is my father?" They knew that Ogaloussa was right.

For it is a saying among them that a man is not really dead until he is forgotten.

Starting Time		Finishing Time	
Reading Time		Reading Rate	
Comprehension		Vocabulary	

Comprehension
— Read the following questions and statements. For each one, put an *x* in the box before the option that contains the most complete or accurate answer. Check your answers in the Answer Key on page 106.

1. Ogaloussa's decision to give the cow's tail to his youngest son was
   □ a. supported by the villagers.
   □ b. strongly debated.
   □ c. resented by his sons.
   □ d. misunderstood by Puli.

2. According to the customs of Kundi, the worst thing people could do to a dead man was to
   □ a. bury him.   □ c. honor him.
   □ b. forget him.   □ d. scorn him.

3. Because Ogaloussa returned from the land of the dead, he was expected to
   □ a. make a cow-tail switch.
   □ b. honor his sons.
   □ c. shave his head.
   □ d. speak a new language.

4. The purpose of the selection is to
   □ a. embarrass a forgetful wife.
   □ b. start a family argument.
   □ c. teach a lesson.
   □ d. describe African customs.

5. The people of Kundi considered it a great honor to be
   □ a. invited to a great feast.
   □ b. recalled from the land of the dead.
   □ c. asked to sing and dance.
   □ d. awarded a braided cow's tail.

6. The cow-tail switch should rightfully have been given to
   □ a. the leader of the village.
   □ b. Ogaloussa's oldest son.
   □ c. Puli.
   □ d. Puli's mother.

7. The decision to search for Ogaloussa was prompted by his
   □ a. youngest son.
   □ b. wife.
   □ c. eldest son.
   □ d. friends.

8. The atmosphere at the beginning of the selection is
   - ☐ a. strained and worried.
   - ☐ b. orderly and peaceful.
   - ☐ c. noisy and troubled.
   - ☐ d. dark and suspicious.

9. Ogaloussa's sons were
   - ☐ a. heartless.
   - ☐ b. forgetful.
   - ☐ c. evil.
   - ☐ d. jealous.

10. The selection is written in the form of a
    - ☐ a. mystery.
    - ☐ b. folktale.
    - ☐ c. short story.
    - ☐ d. biography.

Comprehension Skills

1. recalling specific facts	6. making a judgment
2. retaining concepts	7. making an inference
3. organizing facts	8. recognizing tone
4. understanding the main idea	9. understanding characters
5. drawing a conclusion	10. appreciation of literary forms

Study Skills, Part One—Following is a passage with blanks where words have been omitted. Next to the passage are groups of five words, one group for each blank. Complete the passage by selecting the correct word for each of the blanks.

How to Preview, II

We have seen how previewing is necessary for intelligent reading. The first three steps, as you have read, are (1) read the title, (2) read the subheads, and (3) read the illustrations. Here are the last three steps:

4. Read the Opening Paragraph. The first paragraph is the author's opening, his first opportunity to address the __(1)__ . This paragraph is also called the introductory paragraph because it is precisely that—an introduction to the article or chapter. Opening paragraphs are __(2)__ with different purposes in mind. Some authors announce what they plan to say in the main body of the work. Other authors tell us why they are writing the article or chapter and why it is important for us to read it. Still other authors will do what speakers do—start with a story or anecdote to __(3)__ the stage. That provides the setting or mood they need to present their material.

5. Read the Closing Paragraph. The next step in previewing is to go to the __(4)__ and read the last paragraph. That is the author's last chance to address the reader. If he has any closing remarks or final thoughts, or if he wishes to reemphasize or restate principal thoughts or arguments, he will do it in the closing paragraph. Since it is the closing paragraph, it must express concluding or summarizing thoughts. You'll see what the __(5)__ considers important in his closing paragraph.

6. Skim Through. Finally, before completing your preview, quickly skim the article or chapter to see what else you can __(6)__ . Watch for headings and numbers that indicate important __(7)__ of the author's presentation. You may, for example, learn that the material is divided into four or five major aspects; that knowledge will be helpful when you are reading.

(1)	envelope		reader
	crowd	audience	package
(2)	written		found
	analyzed	used	developed
(3)	set		light
	fill	fix	decorate
(4)	book		middle
	beginning	end	library
(5)	reader		teacher
	author	editor	student
(6)	understand		skim
	learn	teach	know
(7)	additions		reversals
	proofs	introductions	facets

Study Skills, Part Two—Read the study skills passage again, paying special attention to the lesson being taught. Then, without looking back at the passage, complete each sentence below by writing in the missing word or words. Check the Answer Key on page 106 for the answers to Study Skills, Part One, and Study Skills, Part Two.

1. The first paragraph is usually an _____ to the article.

2. Authors use the first paragraph to announce their plans, to give their reason for writing the article, or to provide a _____ .

3. In the concluding paragraph, the author may restate _____ points.

4. In the concluding paragraph, the author may gather the facts in the article, and _____ them.

5. Finally, we should quickly _____ the article one more time to complete the preview.

4 The Grand Canyon by Chopper

by William H. Honan

Vocabulary—The five words below are from the story you are about to read. Study the words and their meanings. Then complete the ten sentences that follow, using one of the five words to fill in the blank in each sentence. Mark your answer by writing the letter of the word on the line before the sentence. Check your answers in the Answer Key on page 106.

A. salvage: rescue

B. perilous: dangerous; hazardous

C. departed: left

D. ambitious: eager

E. wry: drily humorous

_____ 1. Flying a fixed-wing aircraft in the Grand Canyon is more _____ than flying a helicopter.

_____ 2. The author made reservations for a helicopter flight before he _____ from his hotel.

_____ 3. Workers may not be able to _____ anything from a fiery plane crash.

_____ 4. Only the most _____ sightseers sign up for helicopter rides through the Grand Canyon.

_____ 5. Sudden blasts of wind make an aerial trip through the Grand Canyon a _____ journey.

_____ 6. Less _____ pilots would not be interested in flying through the Grand Canyon.

_____ 7. The author noted the lack of flight insurance in a _____ way.

_____ 8. By the time the author _____ the Grand Canyon, he was happy he had taken the helicopter ride.

_____ 9. _____ work in the Grand Canyon is very dangerous.

_____ 10. Dan Nicholson answered the author's questions in a _____ tone.

They don't sell flight insurance at the Grand Canyon heliport.

"The ultimate in Grand Canyon tripping," proclaimed a travel brochure found in my hotel room in Phoenix, Arizona, "is the world-renowned helicopter flight." Being something of a Walter Mitty-type daredevil, I was seized immediately with the fantasy of bobbing around in a newfangled flying machine inside a gusty gorge one mile deep and filled with some of the world's most spectacular obstacles. I was on my way to visit the Grand Canyon anyway, and so I made my reservation by telephone for a helicopter flight.

During the five-hour drive north from Phoenix, however, I began to get cold feet. I recalled a conversation I had during my army days with a couple of army helicopter pilots who had done salvage work in the Grand Canyon after two airliners collided in mid-air and fell into the canyon. The pilots told hair-raising stories of sudden, high-velocity bursts of wind and other conditions that made their assignment perilous.

My misgivings increased just before I reached the Grand Canyon when I passed a huge highway billboard extolling in four-foot-tall letters the **EXCITMENT** of the helicopter ride. If the outfit that flies helicopters through the Grand Canyon can't even spell the word "excitement," I reflected, there's no telling how many loose screws there may be on their choppers.

Arriving at the Grand Canyon tourist office a few minutes later, I asked the young girl behind the counter: "Uh, that helicopter trip . . . just how *dangerous* is it?"

"Oh, not a bit," she cooed.

"Well," I replied, frowning and behaving as though I were privileged to some special knowledge, "they *have* had a few accidents lately, haven't they?" I was just fishing, of course, and therefore was stunned by her reply.

"No, no, not *this* company," she said. "You must have heard about the people who ran the helicopters *before* this company took over. *They* had a crash about every week!"

Thereupon, I decided that the perfect way for me to visit the Grand Canyon was by pack mule. I canceled my reservation and departed to take my first look at the Canyon—from the rim.

On first look, of course, the Grand Canyon is impossible to see. What your eyes report, instead of the Grand Canyon, is a painting, a mural. It simply lacks reality. You confront a vast gorge 18 miles across and 30-odd miles in length, studded with towering buttes and splashed with blue, rose, deep purple, and brown. Everyone knows all about that because everyone has seen the photographs dozens of times. The trouble with looking at it in actuality is that you have nothing to relate it to, nothing to measure it by. What the National Park Service ought to do to help people appreciate the Grand Canyon, I concluded, would be to dump the Empire State Building into it. That would really help us tourists comprehend the extraordinary dimensions of what we are looking at.

After enjoying the sunset from Mojave Point, I started back to my motel room. As I drove past the heliport, I noticed lights in the hangar. I strolled in and soon struck up a conversation with a tall, thin, blond lad of about 25 who told me his name was Mike Antonelli and that he was one of three chopper pilots who worked for Grand Canyon Helicopters. Like the other GCH pilots, he said, he had learned to fly a helicopter in the army and had then flown combat missions in Vietnam. Pretty soon I got around to the question of safety.

"I wouldn't call these flights dangerous," Mike said in the reassuring tone of voice that all pilots seem to adopt. "It's hard to believe it, but a helicopter is actually *safer* than a fixed-wing aircraft." I pricked up my ears at that. "If the engine quits," he continued, "a helicopter has a feature called autorotation. That is, the rotor windmills. It spins freely. And you can glide to a perfectly safe landing. We practice power-off landings all the time. There is *some* risk involved, of course. You get only one pass at where you want to land, but the beauty of a helicopter is that, unlike a fixed-wing aircraft, it can land in a confined area."

Well, I thought to myself, maybe a helicopter is safer than a conventional airplane for flying in the Grand Canyon, but that's like saying a motorscooter is less dangerous than a motorcycle in the Peruvian Andes. Why risk my neck flying *anything* inside the Canyon? Still, I had to admit, I was intrigued. I asked why the company that ran the helicopter service in the Canyon before had had so many accidents.

"They weren't making scenic flights," Mike replied. "They were doing construction work—laying a pipeline across the Canyon in order to bring drinking water over to the South Rim. That was dangerous work. They were using their helicopters to carry pipe and heavy equipment, and they carried close to the maximum load on every trip. Also, they would have to get in much closer to rock formations than we would consider safe."

"What sort of a safety record do you have?" I asked.

"Each of us flies about a dozen trips a day," Mike began, "and in two years we've never had a serious accident. There have been a couple of incidents. Once, when I was landing at the Havasupai Indian Reservation inside the Canyon my rotor struck a wire, but nobody was hurt, and there was only minimal damage. On another occasion a helicopter tipped over out here on landing. Everybody got out safely, but when some fuel spilled out and the fumes hit the hot engine, the helicopter caught fire and burned up."

Mike was forthright enough to admit that, although the company's safety record was fairly good, flying in the Grand Canyon could be treacherous. "Precisely because it's dangerous to a degree," he said, "the FAA discourages private pilots from flying in the Canyon. There are situations that could trick an inexperienced pilot. For example, the North Rim of the Canyon is 1,000 feet higher than the South Rim, and it slopes toward the South Rim. So when you're flying inside the Canyon and look south, you might be above the South Rim and think you're not inside the Canyon and then turn and fly into the north wall. There are some tricky Venturi effects in the Canyon, too—that's where the wind is forced between two buttes and comes out at great velocity. The shadows, too, can throw you if you aren't prepared for them. One minute you're flying along in bright sunlight, and the next you're in the shadow. You can become temporarily blind and experience other perceptual distortions. Flying the Canyon every day, however, we get used to these things. And on the scenic flights we always fly the same routes; so we know what to expect."

I felt Mike had been frank with me, and even if he had not completely dispelled my misgivings, he had captured my imagination. So I signed up for a flight at 10:30 A.M. the next day.

When I returned to the heliport in the morning, I met Dan Nicholson, the chief pilot of Grand Canyon Helicopters, a crisply neat man of about 35 who would take me into the Canyon. I chose the shortest and least expensive of the flights offered—the "Grand View Flight," which would last only 20 minutes and cost $17.50. (More ambitious chopper flyers may tour the whole western portion of the Canyon for $100.)

Nicholson led me and four other passengers to a little, white, French-built Alouette helicopter. (GCH also operates two other smaller Bell helicopters.) A ground attendant buckled our seat belts, and the turbine engine started up with a whine that soon became a scream. The little chopper shook violently. We rose off the ground with a lurch, like a lame duck rising first from one foot and then, a second or two later, from the other. Before we were more than 15 feet in the air, we started to skim forward rapidly. We glided up over the tops of some scrub trees, then ascended more steeply as we approached some telephone lines. The bright sunlight inside the helicopter flickered as the rotors sliced overhead. Nicholson explained that we were doing about 60 mph as we climbed and then would cruise at 80 or 90 mph. We would cover a distance of 25 miles on this trip, descending some 1,500 feet into the Canyon, he explained.

Presently we caught sight of the Canyon—about 50 miles of it from this altitude, or nearly twice what I had seen the day before while standing on the rim. It looked like a sore gash in the earth, the blue and rose colors suggesting a wound of some sort. We were headed for Vishnu Temple, a towering butte of red limestone inside the Canyon, which, if measured from the Canyon floor from which it rises, is the tallest mountain in the state of Arizona.

Then we flew over the rim. What an experience! The earth simply fell away. One moment we were flying at 300 feet; the next at 3,000 feet. I had the sensation of floating. Giant shapes seemed to swim by below. The rock formations of the great Canyon appeared toylike from this height—as though I could reach down and pick them up between two fingers. It was a magical experience.

We began our descent. This gave me a terrifying sinking feeling at first, but, as soon as I realized that I was not simply falling but descending at a controlled rate, I relaxed and began looking around. Visibility from this little bug was superb. I was enclosed in a Plexiglas bubble, unobstructed by any wing or almost any part of the fuselage. I had a clear view around of about 250 degrees. I could look straight up and almost, but not quite, straight down. There were several moments in which I felt I was not riding inside an aircraft but was freely suspended in the air all by myself. The feeling made me clutch my seat with both hands.

We crossed the Colorado River at Grapevine Rapids—it appeared to be a long, bright green snake flecked with white. Then we descended still lower and turned to the left. Ahead were two enormous, red-colored, sheer mountain peaks—Hawkins Butte to the left and Dunn Butte to the right. There was a connecting wall of red limestone between the two, and we were about to fly over it. Nicholson explained that the wall is as tall as a 55-story building. As we sailed over the wall, we hit an updraft and the chopper bounced 10 or 15 feet up in the air. "That's nothing," said Nicholson. "You take a fixed-wing flight if you wanna know what an updraft is really like," he added with a wry smile. Conventional airplanes are more sensitive to wind effects than helicopters, he explained, because they have greater surface area.

Our altimeter was registering 6,000 feet. That put us 3,600 feet above the Canyon floor since the Colorado River here is 2,400 feet above sea level. Way down below Nicholson pointed out a couple of inflated rafts, which appeared to be just shoving off from a beach. We spiraled down 500 feet toward the rafts—an eerie, disorienting motion, even though we were still several thousand feet over their heads.

Then we commenced our climb up out of the Canyon. As before, the pilot did not increase engine power but rather adjusted the pitch of the rotor, and up we went with no seeming increase of energy. We were merely trading a little forward speed for altitude gain, Nicholson explained. We were less than a quarter mile from the south wall, and we could see Kaibab Trail sloping down beneath us. Looking sharply, we saw about a dozen specks moving along the trail. We were too far away to tell whether they were mule riders or hikers. And then up over the rim we came, and suddenly it seemed as though we had returned to the real world, for once again we were not far above the tops of the big pine trees.

We skimmed along over the entrance road, then swooped down over the bright orange hangar of the heliport and dropped to a soft landing—much softer than I have ever experienced in an ordinary airplane. I shook hands with Nicholson and thanked him for a magnificent experience.

Would I recommend helicopter flying in the Grand Canyon? Yes, indeed! Although the parents of small children should bear in mind that they don't sell flight insurance at the Grand Canyon Heliport.

Starting Time		*Finishing Time*	
Reading Time		*Reading Rate*	
Comprehension		*Vocabulary*	

Comprehension— Read the following questions and statements. For each one, put an *x* in the box before the option that contains the most complete or accurate answer. Check your answers in the Answer Key on page 106.

1. Experienced pilots seem to agree that in the Grand Canyon
   □ a. the wind is unpredictable.
   □ b. air travel should be forbidden.
   □ c. helicopters cannot be controlled.
   □ d. salvage work is relatively easy.

2. The author eventually decided that the helicopter tour was
   □ a. perfectly safe.
   □ b. not for him.
   □ c. a reasonable risk.
   □ d. an exciting idea.

3. The author had not considered taking a helicopter ride over the Grand Canyon until he
   □ a. read a billboard advertising Grand Canyon Helicopters.
   □ b. reached his hotel room in Phoenix.
   □ c. talked to Mike.
   □ d. stood on the North Rim of the Canyon.

4. What sentence best expresses the main idea?
   □ a. A helicopter ride is a novel and exciting way to see the Grand Canyon.
   □ b. Helicopter pilots who fly through the Grand Canyon usually get their training in the army.
   □ c. Grand Canyon Helicopters' pilots fly through the Canyon every day.
   □ d. All flights through the Grand Canyon are uninsured.

5. The Grand Canyon seems to
   □ a. require special supervision.
   □ b. frighten most visitors.
   □ c. discourage air travel.
   □ d. boggle the imagination.

6. Which of the following positively confirmed the author's misgivings about helicopters and the Grand Canyon?
   □ a. the two Army helicopter pilots
   □ b. an article he read in a magazine
   □ c. the pilot of Grand Canyon Helicopters
   □ d. the receptionist at the Grand Canyon tourist office

7. Scenic helicopter rides through the Grand Canyon
   □ a. are as dangerous as motorcycle rides in the Peruvian Andes.
   □ b. cost more money than they are worth.
   □ c. should not be attempted by amateur pilots.
   □ d. offer no advantages over other means of exploring the Canyon.

8. In the course of the selection, the author's tone concerning the helicopter ride changed from
   □ a. skeptical to thrilled.
   □ b. idealistic to bitter.
   □ c. bored to excited.
   □ d. frightened to disappointed.

9. Mike and Dan truly believed
   □ a. the author would dislike flying.
   □ b. the FAA should monitor their flights more carefully.
   □ c. all tourists should take helicopter rides through the Canyon.
   □ d. their trips through the Canyon were safe.

10. The author presents his information through
   □ a. questions and answers.
   □ b. lengthy descriptions.
   □ c. careful analysis.
   □ d. official reports.

Comprehension Skills

1. recalling specific facts	*6. making a judgment*
2. retaining concepts	*7. making an inference*
3. organizing facts	*8. recognizing tone*
4. understanding the main idea	*9. understanding characters*
5. drawing a conclusion	*10. appreciation of literary forms*

Study Skills, Part One—Following is a passage with blanks where words have been omitted. Next to the passage are groups of five words, one group for each blank. Complete the passage by selecting the correct word for each of the blanks.

Question the Author

You've probably heard it said that you'll never learn if you don't ask questions.

Why is an inquisitiveness associated with learning? We speak of the student seeking knowledge, or of the __(1)__ mind, and both of those concepts imply asking or questioning.

That is because learning is not a passive process; it is something we *do*. Learning is a(n) __(2)__. We must go after it and seek it out. That is why we say that questioning is part of learning.

Good students question the author following previewing by asking, "What can I expect to learn from this chapter or article? Based on my __(3)__ what are some of the topics likely to be presented? What will the author tell me about this subject?" Questions of that nature frame the subject and provide an __(4)__ to be filled in when reading.

Another thing we hope to discover from questioning is the author's method of presentation. There are many methods an author can use in presenting material. Some may ask questions and answer them, using that __(5)__ to make the subject easier to learn. Some may give details, or describe and illustrate. Others still may compare and contrast. Whatever the method, discover it and put it to use when studying.

In many books the questions are there waiting to be used. Check your textbooks. Are there questions following the chapters? If so, use them during previewing to instill the inquisitiveness so necessary to learning. Those are special questions—they tell us what important points the author really __(6)__ you to learn in each chapter.

Develop the technique of questioning. Try whenever you study to __(7)__ questions you expect to find answered.

| (1) | restless | inactive |
| | trained | inquiring | satisfied |

| (2) | activity | avocation |
| | possession | vacation | accident |

| (3) | education | prereading |
| | attitude | condition | skills |

| (4) | summary | introduction |
| | reason | lecture | outline |

| (5) | material | technique |
| | position | career | review |

| (6) | discovers | avoids |
| | forces | expects | forbids |

| (7) | create | remember |
| | enjoy | distrust | encourage |

Study Skills, Part Two—Read the study skills passage again, paying special attention to the lesson being taught. Then, without looking back at the passage, complete each sentence below by writing in the missing word or words. Check the Answer Key on page 106 for the answers to Study Skills, Part One, and Study Skills, Part Two.

1. In order to learn, it is necessary to _____ .

2. Ask yourself what you expect to _____ from the article.

3. One of your aims should be to discover the author's method of

   _____ .

4. One method the author may use is comparison and _____ .

5. Be sure to check for questions _____ the chapters.

5 Letter Found in a Cement Barrel

by Hayama Yoshiki

Translated by Ivan Morris

Vocabulary—The five words below are from the story you are about to read. Study the words and their meanings. Then complete the ten sentences that follow, using one of the five words to fill in the blank in each sentence. Mark your answer by writing the letter of the word on the line before the sentence. Check your answers in the Answer Key on page 106.

A. spewing: forcing out in a stream; gushing

B. vaguely: faintly

C. furiously: desperately

D. exasperated: irritated

E. din: a mixture of loud and confused noises

_____ 1. Matsudo Yoshizo worked _____ to support his large family.

_____ 2. The factory girl seemed to be _____ out all her emotions in the note she wrote.

_____ 3. Matsudo Yoshizo was _____ by his inability to open the box.

_____ 4. Matsudo Yoshizo seemed _____ disturbed by his wife's seventh pregnancy.

_____ 5. The _____ of machines at the Nomura Cement Company must have been deafening.

_____ 6. The pace set by the cement mixer forced Matsudo Yoshizo to shovel _____ all day long.

_____ 7. When his nose filled with cement Matsudo Yoshizo became quite _____ .

_____ 8. At first Matsudo Yoshizo was only _____ interested in the wooden box.

_____ 9. Matsudo Yoshizo's home was filled with the _____ of children.

_____ 10. At the end of the day the mixer finally stopped _____ out cement.

"But how shall I find his grave to say good-bye to him?"

Matsudo Yoshizo was emptying cement barrels. He managed to keep the cement off most of his body, but his hair and upper lip were covered by a thick gray coating. He desperately wanted to pick his nose and remove the hardened cement which was making the hairs of his nostrils stand stiff like reinforced concrete; but the cement mixer was spewing forth ten loads every minute and he could not afford to fall behind.

His working day lasted for eleven hours and not once did he have time to pick his nose properly. During his brief lunch break he was hungry and had to concentrate on gulping down food. He had hoped to use the afternoon break for cleaning out his nostrils, but when the time came he found that he had to unclog the cement mixer instead. By late afternoon his nose felt as if it were made of plaster of Paris.

The day drew to an end. His arms had become limp with exhaustion, and he had to exert all his strength to move the barrels. As he started to lift one of them, he noticed a small wooden box lying in the cement.

"What's this?" he wondered vaguely, but he could not let curiosity slow down the pace of his work. Hurriedly he shoveled the cement on to the measuring frame, emptied it into the mixing boat, and then began shoveling out more cement again.

"Wait a minute!" he muttered to himself. "Why should there be a box inside a cement barrel?"

He picked up the box and dropped it into the front pocket of his overalls.

"Doesn't weigh much! Can't be much money in it, whatever else there is."

Even this slight pause had made him fall behind in his work, and now he had to shovel furiously to catch up with the cement mixer. Like a wild automaton, he emptied the next barrel and loaded the contents onto a new measuring frame.

Presently the mixer began to slow down and eventually it came to a stop. It was time for Matsudo Yoshizo to knock off for the day. He picked up the rubber hose that was attached to the mixer and made a preliminary attempt at washing his face and hands. Then he hung his lunch box round his neck and trudged back to his tenement. His mind was absorbed with the idea of getting some food into his stomach and, even more important, a powerful cup of distilled rice wine.

He passed the power plant. The construction work was almost finished: soon they would be having electricity. In the distance Mount Keira towered in the evening darkness with its coat of pure white snow. The man's sweaty body was suddenly gripped by the cold, and he began to shiver. Next to where he walked the rough waters of the Kiso River bit into the milky foam with a barking roar.

He thought of the six children who already squirmed about their tenement room, and of the new child who was going to be born as the cold season was coming on, and of his wife who seemed to give birth pell-mell to one baby after another; and he was sick at heart.

"Let's see now," he muttered. "They pay me one yen ninety sen a day, and out of that we have to buy two *shō* of rice at fifty sen, and then we have to pay out another ninety sen for clothing and a place to live. How do they expect me to have enough left over for a drink?"

Then abruptly he remembered the little box in his pocket. He took it out and rubbed it against the seat of his trousers to clean off the cement. Nothing was written on the box. It was securely locked.

"Now, why should anyone want to lock a box like this? He likes to act mysterious, whoever he is."

He hit the box against a stone, but the lid still would not open. Thoroughly exasperated, he threw it down and stepped on it furiously. The box broke and on the ground lay a scrap of paper wrapped in a rag. He picked it up and read:

"I am a factory girl working for the Nomura Cement Company. I sew cement bags. My boyfriend used to work for the same company. His job was to put stones into the crusher. Then on the morning of October 7th just as he was going to put in a big rock he slipped on the mud and fell into the crusher underneath the rock.

"The other men tried to pull him out, but it was no use. He sank down under the rock, just as if he was being drowned. Then the rock and his body were broken to pieces and came out together from the ejector looking like a big flat pink stone. They fell on to the conveyer belt and were carried into the pulverizer. There they were pounded by the huge steel cylinder. I could hear them screaming out some sort of a spell as they were finally crushed to smithereens. Then they were put into the burner and baked into a fine slab of cement.

"His bones, his flesh, his mind had all turned to powder. Yes, my entire boyfriend ended up as cement. All that was left was a scrap of material from his overalls. Today I've been busy sewing a bag into which they'll put him.

"I'm writing this letter two days after he became cement, and when I've finished I'm going to stick it into the barrel.

"Are you a workman, too? If you are, have a heart and send me an answer. What is the cement in this barrel used for? I very much want to know.

"How many barrels of cement did he become? And is it all used in the same place or in different places? Are you a plasterer or a builder?

"I couldn't bear to see him become the corridor of a

theater or the wall of some large mansion. But what on earth can I do to stop it? If you are a workman, please don't use the cement in such a place. . . .

"On second thought, though, it doesn't matter. Use it wherever you want. Wherever he's buried, he'll make a good job of it. He's a good solid fellow and he'll do the right thing wherever he happens to end up.

"He had a very gentle nature, you know. But at the same time he was a brave, husky fellow. He was still young. He'd only just turned twenty-five. I never had time to find out how much he really loved me. And here I am sewing a shroud for him—or rather, a cement bag. Instead of going into a crematorium, he ended up in a rotation kiln. But how shall I find his grave to say good-by to him? I haven't the faintest idea where he's going to be buried, you see. East or west, far or near—there's no way of telling. That's why I want you to send me an answer. If you're a workman, you will answer me, won't you? And in return I'll give you a piece of cloth from his overalls—yes, the piece of cloth this letter's wrapped in. The dust from that rock, the sweat from his body—it's all gone into this cloth. The cloth is all that's left of those overalls he used to wear when he embraced me—oh, how hard he used to embrace me!

"Please do this for me, won't you? I know it's a lot of trouble, but please let me know the date when this cement was used, and the sort of place it was used in and the exact address—and also your own name. And you'll be careful too, won't you? Good-by."

The din of the children once more surged about Matsudo Yoshizo. He glanced at the name and address at the end of the letter and gulped down the rice wine that he had poured into a tea cup.

"I'm going to drink myself silly!" he shouted. "And I'm going to break every damned thing I can lay my hands on."

"I see," said his wife. "So you can afford to get drunk, can you? And what about the children?"

He looked at his wife's bloated stomach and remembered his seventh child.

Starting Time		*Finishing Time*	
Reading Time		*Reading Rate*	
Comprehension		*Vocabulary*	

Comprehension — Read the following questions and statements. For each one, put an *x* in the box before the option that contains the most complete or accurate answer. Check your answers in the Answer Key on page 106.

1. The dead man was the factory girl's
   □ a. brother.
   □ b. boyfriend.
   □ c. fiancé.
   □ d. husband.

2. Matsudo Yoshizo worked steadily because
   □ a. he was a strong and willing worker.
   □ b. he had to keep up with a machine.
   □ c. the thought of the black box made him hurry.
   □ d. he earned more if he worked faster.

3. Because of his modest salary, Matsudo Yoshizo
   □ a. could not afford to buy much rice wine.
   □ b. usually dressed in overalls.
   □ c. was seeking a job in a factory.
   □ d. could not help the factory girl.

4. The selection offers a strong argument in support of the
   □ a. need for automation.
   □ b. dignity of labor.
   □ c. limitation of families.
   □ d. rights of workers.

5. Matsudo Yoshizo's eleven-hour workday is
   □ a. admirable.
   □ b. necessary.
   □ c. inhuman.
   □ d. interesting.

6. There should have been at least
   □ a. another man working with Matsudo Yoshizo.
   □ b. two rest periods in Matsudo Yoshizo's workday.
   □ c. a conveniently located measuring frame.
   □ d. an official to supervise Matsudo Yoshizo's work.

7. The men putting stones into the crusher
   □ a. had more rest periods than other workers.
   □ b. did dangerous work.
   □ c. were warned not to step in the mud.
   □ d. made good money.

8. The thoughts that crossed Matsudo Yoshizo's mind as he walked home from work were
   □ a. hopeful.
   □ b. rebellious.
   □ c. depressing.
   □ d. satisfied.

9. When the factory girl wrote the note, she was feeling
   - ☐ a. courageous.
   - ☐ b. heavy-hearted.
   - ☐ c. irate.
   - ☐ d. peaceful.

10. The selection is written in the form of a
    - ☐ a. short story.
    - ☐ b. biography.
    - ☐ c. diary.
    - ☐ d. mystery.

Comprehension Skills

1. recalling specific facts	6. making a judgment
2. retaining concepts	7. making an inference
3. organizing facts	8. recognizing tone
4. understanding the main idea	9. understanding characters
5. drawing a conclusion	10. appreciation of literary forms

Study Skills, Part One—Following is a passage with blanks where words have been omitted. Next to the passage are groups of five words, one group for each blank. Complete the passage by selecting the correct word for each of the blanks.

How to Concentrate, I

If you have trouble concentrating, consider yourself normal. That is the universal student complaint. And it is not restricted just to students. Everyone at some ___(1)___ finds it hard to concentrate.

Concentrating means giving all of your attention to the issue at hand. The trouble comes from distractions, the inability to shut out ___(2)___ matters and noises.

Are there ways to improve your ability to concentrate? Yes.

1. Increase Motivation. You've no doubt observed that you concentrate more easily on matters about which you are highly motivated. Motivation is one key to concentration. You don't become distracted when you're ___(3)___ interested in something.

Those matters that have some immediate and specific goal motivate people most. We study intently our local *Driver's Manual* when the goal of getting a driver's license is at hand. The goal of passing tomorrow's ___(4)___ often helps students concentrate quite effectively the night before.

Your task in increasing motivation, then, is to set a goal that means enough to help you develop the kind of concentration you need. Even a short-range goal might be ___(5)___ to give you the motivation you need at the moment.

2. Prepare to Study. As simple as that may sound, it ___(6)___ . Prepare yourself properly and completely for the task of studying. Distractions will of course be a bother if you don't arrange to remove them, or to remove yourself from them. No one can concentrate in a busy, noisy room. Try to find a quiet, well-lighted spot equipped with a table and a chair. Seated at the table, upright in the chair, you will be in the ___(7)___ posture for studying and concentrating.

(1)	school		time
	step	position	goal
(2)	harmful		important
	interfering	enjoyable	distant
(3)	falsely		really
	not	somewhat	partially
(4)	time		burden
	plan	place	quiz
(5)	enough		lacking
	harmful	excessive	accepted
(6)	shows		fails
	simplifies	works	hurts
(7)	moderate		worst
	best	only	second

Study Skills, Part Two—Read the study skills passage again, paying special attention to the lesson being taught. Then, without looking back at the passage, complete each sentence below by writing in the missing word or words. Check the Answer Key on page 106 for the answers to Study Skills, Part One, and Study Skills, Part Two.

1. Students are not the only people who have _____ concentrating.

2. Concentrating means giving your exclusive _____ , shutting out everything else.

3. _____ is one key to concentration. We don't become distracted when we're interested.

4. It's easy to concentrate on something when you have a definite _____ in mind.

5. When you prepare to study, find a comfortable, quiet place, free from _____ .

6 | # How We Kept Mother's Day

by Stephen Leacock

Vocabulary—The five words below are from the story you are about to read. Study the words and their meanings. Then complete the ten sentences that follow, using one of the five words to fill in the blank in each sentence. Mark your answer by writing the letter of the word on the line before the sentence. Check your answers in the Answer Key on page 106.

A. notion: idea

B. becoming: attractive

C. appropriate: suitable; fitting

D. reckoned: planned; figured

E. humor: indulge; go along with

_____ 1. A drive to the country seemed like an _____ way to spend Mother's Day.

_____ 2. Mother _____ her family would be late getting home.

_____ 3. The two girls looked quite _____ in their new hats.

_____ 4. Mother knew how to _____ her family.

_____ 5. It seemed _____ that Mother arrange the decorations.

_____ 6. Father liked the _____ of a family fishing trip.

_____ 7. Several local boys apparently found Anne and Mary _____ in their country clothes.

_____ 8. The narrator liked the _____ of celebrating Mother's Day.

_____ 9. The family _____ on making Mother's Day an annual event.

_____ 10. Father insisted that the drive in the country was designed to _____ Mother.

Of all the different ideas that have been started lately, I think that the very best is the notion of celebrating once a year "Mother's Day." I don't wonder that this is becoming such a popular day all over America and I am sure the idea will spread to England too.

It is especially in a big family like ours that such an idea takes hold. So we decided to have a special celebration of Mother's Day. We thought it a fine idea. It made us all realize how much Mother had done for us for years, and all the efforts and sacrifices that she had made for our sake.

It had been the most wonderful day in her life, and there were tears in her eyes.

a definite purpose; and anyway, it turned out that Father had just got a new rod the day before, which made the idea of fishing all the more appropriate, and he said that Mother could use it if she wanted to; in fact, he said it was practically for her, only Mother said she would much rather watch him fish and not try to fish herself.

So we got everything arranged for the trip, and we got Mother to cut up some sandwiches and make up a sort of lunch in case we got hungry, though of course we were to come back home to a big dinner in the middle of the day, just like Christmas or New Year's Day. Mother packed it all up in a basket for us ready to go in the motor.

So we decided that we'd make it a great day, a holiday for all the family, and do everything we could to make Mother happy. Father decided to take a holiday from his office so as to help in celebrating the day, and my sister Anne and I stayed home from college classes, and Mary and my brother Will stayed home from high school.

It was our plan to make it a day just like Christmas or any big holiday, and so we decided to decorate the house with flowers and with mottoes over the mantelpieces, and all that kind of thing. We got Mother to make mottoes and arrange the decorations, because she always does it at Christmas.

The two girls thought it would be a nice thing to dress in our very best for such a big occasion, and so they both got new hats. Mother trimmed both the hats, and they looked fine, and Father had bought four-in-hand silk ties for himself and us boys as a souvenir of the day to remember Mother by. We were going to get Mother a new hat too, but it turned out that she seemed to really like her old gray bonnet better than a new one, and both girls said that it was awfully becoming to her.

Well, after breakfast we had it arranged as a surprise for Mother that we would hire a motor car and take her for a beautiful drive into the country. Mother is hardly ever able to have a treat like that, because we can only afford to keep one maid, and so Mother is busy in the house nearly all the time. And of course the country is so lovely now that it would be just grand for her to have a lovely morning, driving for miles and miles.

But on the very morning of the day we changed the plan a little bit, because it occurred to Father that a thing it would be better to do even than to take Mother for a motor drive would be to take her fishing. Father said that as the car was hired and paid for, we might just as well use it for a drive up into hills where the streams are. As Father said, if you just go out driving without any object, you have a sense of aimlessness, but if you are going to fish, there is a definite purpose in front of you to heighten the enjoyment.

So we all felt that it would be nicer for Mother to have

Well, when the car came to the door, it turned out that there hardly seemed as much room in it as we had supposed, because we hadn't reckoned on Father's fishing basket and the rods and the lunch, and it was plain enough that we couldn't all get in.

Father said not to mind him, he said that he could just as well stay home, and that he was sure that he could put in the time working in the garden; he said that there was a lot of rough dirty work that he could do, like digging a trench for the garbage, that would save hiring a man, and so he said that he'd stay home; he said that we were not to let the fact of his not having had a real holiday for three years stand in our way; he wanted us to go right ahead and be happy and have a big day, and not to mind him. He said that he could plug away all day, and in fact he said he'd been a fool to think there'd be any holiday for him.

But of course we all felt that it would never do to let Father stay home, especially as we knew he would make trouble if he did. The two girls, Anne and Mary, would gladly have stayed and helped the maid get dinner, only it seemed such a pity to, on a lovely day like this, having their new hats. But they both said that Mother had only to say the word, and they'd gladly stay home and work. Will and I would have dropped out, but unfortunately we wouldn't have been any use in getting the dinner.

So in the end it was decided that Mother would stay home and just have a lovely restful day round the house, and get the dinner. It turned out anyway that Mother doesn't care for fishing, and also it was just a little bit cold and fresh out of doors, though it was lovely and sunny, and Father was rather afraid that Mother might take cold if she came.

He said he would never forgive himself if he dragged Mother round the country and let her take a severe cold at a time when she might be having a beautiful rest. He said it was our duty to try and let Mother get all the rest and quiet that she could, after all that she had done for all of us, and he said that that was principally why he had fallen in with this idea of a fishing trip, so as to give Mother a little quiet. He said that young people seldom realize how much quiet means to people who are getting old. As to himself, he could still stand the racket, but he was glad to shelter Mother from it.

So we all drove away with three cheers for Mother, and Mother stood and watched us from the verandah for as long as she could see us, and Father waved his hand back to her every few minutes till he hit his hand on the back edge of the car, and then said that he didn't think that Mother could see us any longer.

Well, we had the loveliest day up among the hills that you could possibly imagine, and Father caught such big specimens that he felt sure that Mother couldn't have landed them anyway, if she had been fishing for them, and Will and I fished too, though we didn't get so many as Father, and the two girls met quite a lot of people that they knew as we drove along, and there were some young men friends of theirs that they met along the stream and talked to, and so we all had a splendid time.

It was quite late when we got back, nearly seven o'clock in the evening, but Mother had guessed that we would be late, so she had kept back the dinner so as to have it just nicely ready and hot for us. Only first she had to get towels and soap for Father and clean things for him to put on, because he always gets so messed up with fishing, and that kept Mother busy for a little while, that and helping the girls get ready.

But at last everything was ready, and we sat down to the grandest kind of dinner—roast turkey and all sorts of things like on Christmas Day. Mother had to get up and down a good bit during the meal fetching things back

and forward, but at the end Father noticed it and said she simply musn't do it, that he wanted her to spare herself and he got up and fetched the walnuts over from the sideboard himself.

The dinner lasted a long while, and was great fun, and when it was over all of us wanted to help clear the things up and wash the dishes, only Mother said that she would really much rather do it, and so we let her, because we wanted just for once to humor her.

It was quite late when it was all over, and when we all kissed Mother before going to bed, she said it had been the most wonderful day in her life, and I think there were tears in her eyes. So we all felt awfully repaid for all that we had done.

Stephen Leacock ranks as the most popular humorist in Canadian literature, although he is also well known for his serious works and was a distinguished professor of political science. Most of his humorous works poke fun at everyday people and events by treating them with mock seriousness; he also often wrote in humorous imitation of other author's styles. Many of Leacock's essays and short stories first appeared in magazines and newspapers. The first of many collections of humorous works was published in 1910. Leacock was born in 1869 in Swanmore, England. He moved to a farm in Ontario, Canada, when he was six years old and lived in Canada until his death in 1944.

Starting Time		Finishing Time	
Reading Time		Reading Rate	
Comprehension		Vocabulary	

Comprehension— Read the following questions and statements. For each one, put an *x* in the box before the option that contains the most complete or accurate answer. Check your answers in the Answer Key on page 106.

1. At the end of the dinner Father
   □ a. got the walnuts.
   □ b. showed Mother the fish he had caught.
   □ c. thanked Mother for cooking the meal.
   □ d. told the children to go to bed.

2. Mother's Day was created to be a
   □ a. business holiday.
   □ b. replacement for Christmas.
   □ c. day of recognition.
   □ d. holiday from school.

3. Mother decided to stay home because
   □ a. she wanted to help the maid.
   □ b. she was afraid of catching cold.
   □ c. there wasn't enough room in the car for everyone.
   □ d. Father's plans to go fishing angered her.

4. The selection is meant to be
   □ a. offensive.   □ c. controversial.
   □ b. educational.   □ d. humorous.

5. Father loved to
   □ a. pamper Mother.
   □ b. spend time with his children.
   □ c. fish.
   □ d. get out of the house.

6. The reader first suspects that Mother's Day would be a busy work day for Mother when the
   □ a. children asked her to do the mottoes and decorations.
   □ b. girls bought new hats.
   □ c. boys bought silk ties to remember her by.
   □ d. decision was made to organize a fishing outing.

7. Internal evidence suggests that the events of the selection took place in the
   ☐ a. early 1800s. ☐ c. early 1900s.
   ☐ b. middle 1800s. ☐ d. middle 1900s.

8. Father's offer to stay home was
   ☐ a. an obvious strategy to get his way.
   ☐ b. an expression of genuine concern.
   ☐ c. reasonable, considering the work he had to do.
   ☐ d. his contribution to Mother's Day.

9. Mother is portrayed as
   ☐ a. demanding. ☐ c. accommodating.
   ☐ b. foolish. ☐ d. athletic.

10. The expression "he could plug away all day" means that he could
    ☐ a. putter around all day.
    ☐ b. work doggedly all day.
    ☐ c. lounge around all day.
    ☐ d. mope around all day.

Comprehension Skills

1. recalling specific facts
2. retaining concepts
3. organizing facts
4. understanding the main idea
5. drawing a conclusion
6. making a judgment
7. making an inference
8. recognizing tone
9. understanding characters
10. appreciation of literary forms

Study Skills, Part One—Following is a passage with blanks where words have been omitted. Next to the passage are groups of five words, one group for each blank. Complete the passage by selecting the correct word for each of the blanks.

How to Concentrate, II

We've seen two techniques that we can use to improve concentration. They involve (1) increasing motivation, and (2) preparing to study. Here are three other techniques:

3. Set a Time. Have you ever noticed how timing brings out peak efficiency? Almost every athletic event is closely timed; or else the participants are competing against time. For instance, in track events the winner's time generates as much interest as does the place in which she ___(1)___ . Timing is a natural incentive to competitive athletes— they can't resist the ___(2)___ . You can make use of your sense of competition when you have an assignment to complete or a lesson to study. Set a time for the completion of the task. Your inclination to beat the ___(3)___ may inspire the sustained concentration you need. Timing, put simply, builds concentration.

4. Pace the Assignment. Trying to do too much too soon will destroy concentration, not increase it. We know that we cannot sustain full concentration for very long ___(4)___ , especially when we're not in the habit. When an assignment is long, involved, and complex, it's best not to try to ___(5)___ it at one sitting. Segment the task into twenty-minute parcels and spread out the periods of study. Returning to an ___(6)___ task makes it easier to regain concentration, because we want to see the job completed. That desire to get the job done helps build the kind of concentration we need.

5. Organize the Task. One major reason students can't concentrate is that their assignment is unplanned and vague. When that is the case, the assignment itself is a distraction. Through the skills of Previewing and Questioning you should be able to organize the assignment into a series

(1)   finishes   stumbles
        begins   races   lives

(2)   challenge   warmup
        glory   event   injury

(3)   others   system
        enemy   clock   competition

(4)   periods   confinements
        sessions   attempts   skills

(5)   understand   delay
        complete   sustain   ignore

(6)   overlooked   agreeable
        understood   unfinished   optimistic

of ___(7)___ and specific tasks. List exactly what you wish to learn or accomplish in the designated periods of study. Then set up a time framework and stick to it.

(7)   related   ordinary
     assigned   difficult   remembered

Study Skills, Part Two—Read the study skills passage again, paying special attention to the lesson being taught. Then, without looking back at the passage, complete each sentence below by writing in the missing word or words. Check the Answer Key on page 106 for the answers to Study Skills, Part One, and Study Skills, Part Two.

1. To help concentration, it is suggested that you set a _____ for completion of the assignment.

2. It is natural to try and complete the task in a _____ period of time than was suggested.

3. If an assignment is very long, divide it into sections, and _____ out the periods of study.

4. It is important to organize the assignment into several definite _____ .

5. Before you begin, _____ what you want to accomplish in the following period of study.

7 | Coming of Age on City Streets

by Patricia Hersch

Vocabulary—The five words below are from the story you are about to read. Study the words and their meanings. Then complete the ten sentences that follow, using one of the five words to fill in the blank in each sentence. Mark your answer by writing the letter of the word on the line before the sentence. Check your answers in the Answer Key on page 107.

A. nocturnal: taking place at night

B. blatant: obvious; conspicuous

C. lucrative: financially rewarding; profitable

D. implement: carry out

E. invulnerable: incapable of being injured

_____ 1. AIDS-prevention programs for street kids are difficult to _____ .

_____ 2. Drug use is _____ in some parts of New York City.

_____ 3. Neither male nor female prostitutes are _____ to AIDS.

_____ 4. Young runaways see prostitution as a _____ occupation.

_____ 5. The _____ life of many street kids is filled with crack, pimps, and unsafe sex.

_____ 6. Street kids know that any legitimate job they could get would not be nearly as _____ as hustling.

_____ 7. The former prostitute appeared to feel _____ to AIDS.

_____ 8. Some young street kids already show _____ signs of AIDS.

_____ 9. Workers in the Covenant House van make their _____ rounds in hopes of helping street kids.

_____ 10. Shelter workers have tried to _____ programs to pass out free bleach to intravenous drug users.

Homeless kids survive any way they can. Their bodies usually become the currency of exchange.

Each night at 10 o'clock, a van leaves Covenant House, New York City's largest shelter for runaway children, and heads into the nocturnal world of homeless teens. Until 5 A.M., as the van cruises the streets, workers offer lemonade or hot chocolate, bologna sandwiches and cookies to children of the night. Sometimes the kids just want food. Other times they want medical care, protection, or a place to sleep. At all times, their habits and associates place them in extraordinary danger of contracting AIDS. The Covenant House staff wants to build trust and wean the kids from the streets. Reaching them has always been a challenge. Now, it's an emergency.

At the invitation of Anne Donahue, who runs the Covenant House outreach program, I volunteer to help out in a van one night. One of our first visitors is Juan, age 19. He is familiar to the van crew; when he was 14, his parents threw him out of the house because he was gay, and in the course of unsuccessful foster-home placements, he was in and out of Covenant House 14 times. On the streets, he bartered sex for companionship and money. Juan had been most recently seen in January 1987. He was working then in a gay bathhouse and came to the van complaining of swollen glands. He was never diagnosed; he did not stay for assessment. Tonight Juan appears again. His glands are so large that they protrude from his neck, so swollen that he cannot sleep lying down. Exhausted, he falls asleep in the van while talking to me. We bring him back to Covenant House. I learn later that he left before seeing a doctor. Does he have mono? AIDS-related complex? Who knows?

William, 19, and Susan, 17, walk by at 1 A.M., pushing their 6-month-old child in a stroller among the drug dealers, hustlers, and addicts. Susan continues to walk with the baby as William hustles nearby, peddling sex to male customers. William is not gay, but he needs the money to buy diapers and food for his baby. Perhaps later he will make love to Susan.

At 4 A.M. Dolly, 19, and Angela, 21, arrive, eager for cookies and lemonade, and engagingly humorous with John and Rick, the regular workers on the van. Long-haired and gorgeous, decked out in miniskirts and snug, low-cut blouses, they brag that it's been a good night, lots of tricks. Dolly and Angela, like the other "girls" nearby, are really men, their full breasts the result of bootlegged hormone shots. Boys as young as 14 buy hormones that they inject, often with shared needles. As we swing around the block on our way to the next section, we pass Dolly and Angela again. This time they don't see us. They are stooped over, doing crack. In the short time we were gone a drug peddler came by, part of the blatant trafficking we see everywhere we go. Crack is widely available and openly used. The tiny broken glass vials glisten wherever light hits the pavement.

Each section of the city holds new horrors. There are children everywhere. Block after block, I see female prostitutes, some as young as 12 years old, dressed in G-strings, stiletto heels, and not much else. They're bizarre caricatures of little girls playing dress-up as they work to turn 8 to 10 tricks a night. Boys too young to shave are dressed in the most exaggerated stereotypes of gayness. No one has helped them to understand what it means to be homosexual, nor offered support and positive models for the realities of their sexual preferences. So here they are, being whisked into cars by men with money, wandering hands and, most likely, wives and children at home. Wherever we turn, teenagers are being used for sexual recreation by men—lots of men—in cars, in subway stations and bus stations, in sleazy hotels, in alleys and—although I do not see it, I am told—right here on the streets.

Donahue cannot understand why the men, the "johns" who purchase sex, are not scared of contracting AIDS. "They've got to know that they are sleeping with kids who have been all over the place. I talked to a guy, 25 years old, who'd been hustling since he was 14. He has AIDS, but he's going through denial and still doesn't use condoms. I asked him about the johns. Don't they want condoms? He answered, 'If they wanted safe sex, do you think they would be out on 42nd Street? They want fantasies. . . . Condoms aren't part of fantasies. AIDS has no impact on what's going on in the streets.' "

Not true. AIDS has a potentially disastrous effect on what is going on in the streets, particularly in inner cities where sex, drugs, and poverty cross paths that often lead out to the suburbs and all across the country. Many of these runaway and homeless adolescents, between 20,000 and 40,000 in New York City, up to 1.2 million nationwide, are caught at the juncture of risks.

Sex more than anything puts runaway kids at risk for AIDS. Homeless kids survive any way they can. Their bodies usually become the currency of exchange. Many program directors believe that any kid on the street for a month will have to turn to prostitution. They don't have alternatives. Runaway girls, scared and alone, are welcomed by pimps who watch for them as they arrive at bus and train stations. They offer them a roof over their heads, a "caring adult," clothes, makeup, and promises of love and belonging.

Jim Kennedy, a physician and medical director of Covenant House, finds that young girls are being infected with Human Immunodeficiency Virus (HIV) just by having sex with new boyfriends, the guys who take them in when their families throw them out. "Even if these girls never end up working as prostitutes, they are at risk when they have sex with the drug-abusing guys who control the street life of local neighborhoods," he says. Last summer, he tested four girls who fit this description. Three tested HIV-positive. One of the three is pregnant.

For many male runaways, hustling proves too lucrative to resist. As psychologist Nick Lestardo, director of Larkin Street Services in San Francisco, explains, "Male hustling is a good way to make $75 to $200 a night. Many of these boys have already been sexually abused. They realize nobody will hire a 15-year-old. They hear, 'It's not so horrible.' Twenty-five bucks for ten minutes sounds like a lot of money to kids."

Kathie, 19, a former prostitute and a street kid since she was 12, says, "Anywhere out here, there are ways to make money. Legitimate work? No. There's no doors opened to us. . . . How are you going to be able to hold down a job if you have no high school diploma, if you're not able to take a shower every day, if you don't have clean clothes to wear to work? And let's say you came out here because of 'certain circumstances' at home. You're scared out here. You know, what gets me upset is that a lot of these businesspeople think that when they see a kid sleeping on a train, or they see a kid hanging out all the time, they think it's 'cause they wanna be. Now that I'm older, that's not how I see it. These kids are each crying in their own special way. They don't wanna be like that, but their parents don't want them."

These kids may be street tough and sexually experienced but that does not mean they are sexually aware. For example, Kathie, ex-prostitute, sex-show performer, crack user, lives with a man who spends part of his time with other women, including one who is bearing his child. Kathie does not use condoms and airily dismisses AIDS: "I know I ain't got it. I got confidence in myself." She has a different theory about the other kids who live on the streets. "I think they know about AIDS but they ignore it. They say, 'Well, if I die, then I won't have to worry about pain because I feel when you die you have peace. . . . There is nothing to worry about anymore.' But when you live on the streets you have to worry every day."

Outreach and shelter workers do worry about the homeless teenagers and their futures. They are working to design and implement educational programs that alert the kids to the dangers of AIDS and that teach them how to protect themselves.

The obstacles to success are enormous because the children have so many problems. They are elusive, highly stressed, and exhausted. They think they are invulnerable, and, like most adolescents, they don't think beyond today.

"They're all doing crack down at the piers—the transvestites and the gay boys and many of the girls too," says Trudee Able-Peterson, director of the Streetwork Project, an outreach program of the Victims Services Agency in New York. "When they've had a particularly bad day, too much crack, and they haven't slept for three days, they come in and say, 'I must have AIDS, do you think I should get tested? You think my lover has it?' They don't know enough about AIDS and you tell them and they forget. And you tell them again and you give them a handful of condoms. That's a real crackland down in the Village. It's the kind of drug where you lose yourself. So many of them are so high that . . . they push it [AIDS] away."

The shelters and agencies that work with these young people are trying whatever might work. They hand out condoms and flyers showing how to use them correctly. Graphic information about sex is dispensed on the street, and bottles of bleach are given to intravenous drug abusers.

The educators are innovative, honest, open, and desperate. Not one person I interviewed believes they are making a substantial change in the behavior of this population. Why? The teens won't remember; they will reason it is OK to have sex with friends; some girls want to get pregnant; their johns give them more money if they don't use a condom. Mostly, though, there are so many ways to die every day on the street that they cannot focus on something that may kill them years from now.

As these children get sick, who will comfort them? Able-Peterson recently wondered aloud in a speech before the Women's Legislative Caucus in New York: "Who will visit them in the hospital, bring them cards and candy, answer the questions about death and God their desperate eyes will ask? Where will they sleep between hospital visits? On a train? In Penn Station? Who will attend the funerals and weep beside their graves? Who will bury our children?"

The workers are trying to steel themselves. Almost none of the country's shelters for runaways have on-site medical facilities. Kennedy says he will provide hospice care at Covenant House if they have no other place to go.

Meanwhile, Anne Donahue and the Covenant House van travel the streets by night. A terrible sense of urgency propels her. If she can reach a kid one day sooner, a kid who is not yet infected, the youth may be spared one all-important day of risk. "The key to getting through to these children is to move slowly and not push them, to build a relationship," she says. "It's like we're racing against time, but we're not allowed to run."

Starting Time		Finishing Time	
Reading Time		Reading Rate	
Comprehension		Vocabulary	

Comprehension — Read the following questions and statements. For each one, put an *x* in the box before the option that contains the most complete or accurate answer. Check your answers in the Answer Key on page 107.

1. The Covenant House van cruises the streets from
   - ☐ a. 8 P.M. to 8 A.M.
   - ☐ b. 10 P.M. to 5 A.M.
   - ☐ c. midnight to 8 A.M.
   - ☐ d. 8 A.M. to 8 P.M.

2. The Covenant House van offers street kids
   - ☐ a. employment.
   - ☐ b. financial support.
   - ☐ c. psychiatric counseling.
   - ☐ d. practical help.

3. Boys take bootlegged hormone shots in order to
   - ☐ a. protect themselves against AIDS.
   - ☐ b. stave off feelings of hunger and sleepiness.
   - ☐ c. increase their strength.
   - ☐ d. swell their breasts.

4. The street kids of New York City are
   - ☐ a. not productive members of society.
   - ☐ b. alienated from all authority figures.
   - ☐ c. in extreme danger.
   - ☐ d. tougher than they appear to be.

5. Many of the street kids the van workers see will eventually
   - ☐ a. contract AIDS.
   - ☐ b. be reunited with their families.
   - ☐ c. become pimps.
   - ☐ d. find legitimate jobs.

6. Education about AIDS
   - ☐ a. only serves to frighten young people.
   - ☐ b. would keep kids off the streets.
   - ☐ c. needs to be targeted at parents.
   - ☐ d. is not enough.

7. Kids who become prostitutes do not care about
   - ☐ a. the long-term consequences of their actions.
   - ☐ b. attracting customers.
   - ☐ c. making money.
   - ☐ d. pleasing their pimps.

8. When speaking about the problems of dealing with street kids, shelter workers sound
   - ☐ a. pessimistic.
   - ☐ b. insensitive.
   - ☐ c. naive.
   - ☐ d. hopeful.

9. Most street kids are
   - ☐ a. happy and carefree.
   - ☐ b. deeply troubled.
   - ☐ c. content with their lives.
   - ☐ d. terribly scared about AIDS.

10. To strengthen her message about street kids, the author uses
   - ☐ a. literary analogies.
   - ☐ b. government reports.
   - ☐ c. individual examples.
   - ☐ d. historical comparisons.

Comprehension Skills

1. recalling specific facts	6. making a judgment
2. retaining concepts	7. making an inference
3. organizing facts	8. recognizing tone
4. understanding the main idea	9. understanding characters
5. drawing a conclusion	10. appreciation of literary forms

Study Skills, Part One — Following is a passage with blanks where words have been omitted. Next to the passage are groups of five words, one group for each blank. Complete the passage by selecting the correct word for each of the blanks.

How to Remember

Just as there are ways to help concentration, there are techniques we can ___(1)___ to help us remember what we study. Here are three of those techniques.

1. Plan to Remember. That is so obvious that we tend to overlook its value, but it works. Tell yourself that you want to remember something and you will. For example,

(1)   create   adjust
        forget   employ   discard

if you are like most people, you have trouble recalling the name of someone you have just met. The next time you're ___(2)___, plan to remember the person's name. Say to yourself, "I'll listen carefully. I'll repeat the name to be sure I have it. I *will* remember it." You'll find there's nothing to it; you'll probably remember that name for the rest of your life.

Many of us complain that we have short memories, but the truth is we simply don't try to or plan to remember—we don't program our memories. From now on, make up your mind before you read or study that you ___(3)___ to, and will, remember.

2. Review the Material. Most forgetting occurs shortly after the learning has been done. More new material crowds out what information we've just studied, and we have trouble recalling that information. The problem of too much information can be overcome by reviewing. A review, by definition, is not a total rereading of the ___(4)___ assignment. In fact, the technique of previewing, which you have previously learned, is actually reviewing in advance; hence, you already know what reviewing is and how to do it. Previewing again and recalling your ___(5)___ will give you enough of a review to help you remember.

3. Look for Principles. You cannot remember everything. When you try to, you end up remembering nothing. Instead of looking at the assignment as a voluminous collection of ___(6)___, all of which must be remembered, generalize the subject into a few major ideas, or principles, that you can easily recall. You will find that technique to be especially effective in studying for quizzes and exams.

When you try to remember every last fact in a lesson or a book, you actually ___(7)___ retention and waste time.

(2)	praised		worried
	forgotten	introduced	nervous

(3)		need	hate
	want	like	begin

(4)	entire		preceding
	partial	section	final

(5)	statements		questions
	skills	announcements	methods

(6)	experiences		opinions
	facts	goals	results

(7)	maximize		ignore
	attract	conduct	minimize

Study Skills, Part Two—Read the study skills passage again, paying special attention to the lesson being taught. Then, without looking back at the passage, complete each sentence below by writing in the missing word or words. Check the Answer Key on page 107 for the answers to Study Skills, Part One, and Study Skills, Part Two.

1. If you make an effort and _____ to remember, you will.

2. Most of us have never _____ this simple technique.

3. A good way to prevent forgetting what we read is to _____ the material.

4. To remember important points, repeat the technique of _____ again.

5. Don't try to remember everything. _____ the subject into a few major ideas which you can easily recall.

8 Jonathan Livingston Seagull

by Richard Bach

Vocabulary—The five words below are from the story you are about to read. Study the words and their meanings. Then complete the ten sentences that follow, using one of the five words to fill in the blank in each sentence. Mark your answer by writing the letter of the word on the line before the sentence. Check your answers in the Answer Key on page 107.

A. chummed: fished by scattering ground-up fish on the water as bait

B. falter: perform unsteadily; stumble

C. deliberately: intentionally

D. wearily: tiredly

E. drab: dull and dreary

_____ 1. The flock found breakfast by following fishing boats as they _____ .

_____ 2. Jonathan was not content to live the _____ , predictable life of an ordinary seagull.

_____ 3. At the end of a day of experimenting, Jonathan flew _____ back to his flock.

_____ 4. Fishing boats often _____ the waters near Jonathan's home.

_____ 5. From a height of 2,000 feet, Jonathan began a vertical descent with his forewings _____ tucked in.

_____ 6. Most seagulls never engaged in activities that would cause them to _____ or stall.

_____ 7. Jonathan found the life of most seagulls _____ .

_____ 8. After discovering the secret to high-speed flight, Jonathan _____ but happily went to spread the word to his flock.

_____ 9. Jonathan would sometimes _____ during his practice sessions, but he refused to stop experimenting.

_____ 10. On many mornings Jonathan _____ skipped breakfast.

It was morning, and the new sun sparkled gold across the ripples of a gentle sea.

A mile from shore a fishing boat chummed the water, and the word for Breakfast Flock flashed through the air, till a crowd of a thousand seagulls came to dodge and fight for bits of food. It was another busy day beginning.

But way off alone, out

We can lift ourselves out of ignorance and find ourselves creatures of excellence.

by himself beyond boat and shore, Jonathan Livingston Seagull was practicing. A hundred feet in the sky he lowered his webbed feet, lifted his beak, and strained to hold a painful hard twisting curve through his wings. The curve meant that he would fly slowly, and now he slowed until the wind was a whisper in his face, until the ocean stood still beneath him. He narrowed his eyes in fierce concentration, held his breath, forced one . . . single . . . more . . . inch . . . of . . . curve. . . . Then his feathers ruffled, he stalled and fell.

Seagulls, as you know, never falter, never stall. To stall in the air is for them disgrace and it is dishonor.

But Jonathan Livingston Seagull, unashamed, stretching his wings again in that trembling hard curve—slowing, slowing, and stalling once more—was no ordinary bird.

Most gulls don't bother to learn more than the simplest facts of flight—how to get from shore to food and back again. For most gulls, it is not flying that matters, but eating. For this gull, though, it was not eating that mattered, but flight. More than anything else, Jonathan Livingston Seagull loved to fly.

This kind of thinking, he found, is not the way to make one's self popular with other birds. Even his parents were dismayed as Jonathan spent whole days alone, making hundreds of low-level glides, experimenting.

He didn't know why, for instance, but when he flew at altitudes less than half his wingspan above the water, he could stay in the air longer, with less effort. His glides ended not with the usual feet-down splash into the sea, but with a long flat wake as he touched the surface with his feet tightly streamlined against his body. When he began sliding in to feet-up landings on the beach, then pacing the length of his slide in the sand, his parents were very much dismayed indeed.

"Why, Jon, *why?"* his mother asked. "Why is it so hard to be like the rest of the flock, Jon? Why can't you leave low flying to the pelicans, the albatross? Why don't you *eat?* Son, you're bone and feathers!"

"I don't mind being bone and feathers, Mom. I just want to know what I can do in the air and what I can't, that's all. I just want to know."

"See here, Jonathan," said his father, not unkindly. "Winter isn't far away. Boats will be few, and the surface fish will be swimming deep. If you must study, then study food, and how to get it. This flying business is all very well, but you can't eat a glide, you know. Don't you forget that the reason you fly is to eat."

Jonathan nodded obediently. For the next few days he tried to behave like the other gulls; he really tried, screeching and fighting with the flock around the piers and fishing boats, diving on scraps of fish and bread. But he couldn't make it work.

It's all so pointless, he thought, deliberately dropping a hard-won anchovy to a hungry old gull chasing him. I could be spending all this time learning to fly. There's so much to learn!

It wasn't long before Jonathan Gull was off by himself again, far out at sea, hungry, happy, learning.

The subject was speed, and in a week's practice he learned more about speed than the fastest gull alive.

From a thousand feet, flapping his wings as hard as he could, he pushed over into a blazing steep dive toward the waves, and learned why seagulls don't make blazing steep power-dives. In just six seconds he was moving seventy miles per hour, the speed at which one's wing goes unstable on the upstroke.

Time after time it happened. Careful as he was, working at the very peak of his ability, he lost control at high speed.

Climb to a thousand feet. Full power straight ahead first, then push over, flapping, to a vertical dive. Then, every time, his left wing stalled on an upstroke, he'd roll violently left, stall his right wing recovering, and flick like fire into a wild tumbling spin to the right.

He couldn't be careful enough on that upstroke. Ten times he tried, and all ten times, as he passed through seventy miles per hour, he burst into a churning mass of feathers, out of control, crashing down into the water.

The key, he thought at last, dripping wet, must be to hold the wings still at high speeds—to flap up to fifty and then hold the wings still.

From two thousand feet he tried again, rolling into his dive, beak straight down, wings full out and stable from the moment he passed fifty miles per hour. It took tremendous strength, but it worked. In ten seconds he had blurred through ninety miles per hour. Jonathan had set a world speed record for seagulls!

But victory was short-lived. The instant he began his pullout, the instant he changed the angle of his wings, he snapped into that same terrible uncontrolled disaster, and at ninety miles per hour it hit him like dynamite. Jonathan Seagull exploded in midair and smashed down into a brick-hard sea.

When he came to, it was well after dark, and he floated in moonlight on the surface of the ocean. His wings were ragged bars of lead, but the weight of failure was even heavier on his back. He wished, feebly, that the weight could be just enough to drag him gently down to the bottom, and end it all.

As he sank low in the water, a strange hollow voice

sounded within him. There's no way around it. I am a seagull. I am limited by my nature. If I were meant to learn so much about flying, I'd have charts for brains. If I were meant to fly at speed, I'd have a falcon's short wings, and live on mice instead of fish. My father was right. I must forget this foolishness. I must fly home to the Flock and be content as I am, as a poor limited seagull.

The voice faded, and Jonathan agreed. The place for a seagull at night is on shore, and from this moment forth, he vowed, he would be a normal gull. It would make everyone happier.

He pushed wearily away from the dark water and flew toward the land, grateful for what he had learned about work-saving low-altitude flying.

But no, he thought. I am done with the way I was, I am done with everything I learned. I am a seagull like every other seagull, and I will fly like one. So he climbed painfully to a hundred feet and flapped his wings harder, pressing for shore.

He felt better for his decision to be just another one of the flock. There would be no ties now to the force that had driven him to learn, there would be no more challenge and no more failure. And it was pretty, just to stop thinking, and fly through the dark, toward the lights above the beach.

Dark! The hollow voice cracked in alarm. *Seagulls never fly in the dark!*

Jonathan was not alert to listen. It's pretty, he thought. The moon and the lights twinkling on the water, throwing out little beacon-trails through the night, and all so peaceful and still. . . .

Get down! Seagulls never fly in the dark! If you were meant to fly in the dark, you'd have the eyes of an owl! You'd have charts for brains! You'd have a falcon's short wings!

There in the night, a hundred feet in the air, Jonathan Livingston Seagull—blinked. His pain, his resolutions, vanished.

Short wings. *A falcon's short wings!*

That's the answer! What a fool I've been! All I need is a tiny little wing, all I need is to fold most of my wings and fly on just the tips alone! *Short wings!*

He climbed two thousand feet above the black sea, and without a moment for thought of failure and death, he brought his forewings tightly in to his body, left only the narrow swept daggers of his wingtips extended into the wind, and fell into a vertical dive.

The wind was a monster roar at his head. Seventy miles per hour, ninety, a hundred and twenty and faster still. The wing-strain now at a hundred and forty miles per hour wasn't nearly as hard as it had been before at seventy, and with the faintest twist of his wingtips he eased out of the dive and shot above the waves, a gray cannonball under the moon.

He closed his eyes to slits against the wind and rejoiced. A hundred forty miles per hour! And under control! If I dive from five thousand feet instead of two thousand, I wonder how fast. . . .

His vows of a moment before were forgotten, swept away in that great swift wind. Yet he felt guiltless, breaking the promises he had made himself. Such promises are only for the gulls that accept the ordinary. One who has touched excellence in his learning has no need of that kind of promise.

By sunup, Jonathan Gull was practicing again. From five thousand feet the fishing boats were specks in the flat blue water, Breakfast Flock was a faint cloud of dust motes, circling.

He was alive, trembling ever so slightly with delight, proud that his fear was under control. Then without ceremony he hugged in his forewings, extended his short, angled wingtips, and plunged directly toward the sea. By the time he passed four thousand feet he had reached terminal velocity, the wind was a solid beating wall of sound against which he could move no faster. He was flying now straight down, at two hundred fourteen miles per hour. He swallowed, knowing that if his wings unfolded at that speed he'd be blown into a million tiny shreds of seagull. But the speed was power, and the speed was joy, and the speed was pure beauty.

He began his pullout at a thousand feet, wingtips thudding and blurring in that gigantic wind, the boat and the crowd of gulls tilting and growing meteor-fast, directly in his path.

He couldn't stop; he didn't know yet even how to turn at that speed.

Collision would be instant death.

And so he shut his eyes.

It happened that morning, then, just after sunrise, that Jonathan Livingston Seagull fired directly through the center of Breakfast Flock, ticking off two hundred twelve miles per hour, eyes closed, in a great roaring shriek of wind and feathers. The Gull of Fortune smiled upon him this once, and no one was killed.

By the time he had pulled his beak straight up into the sky he was still scorching along at a hundred and sixty miles per hour. When he had slowed to twenty and stretched his wings again at last, the boat was a crumb on the sea, four thousand feet below.

His thought was triumph. Terminal velocity! A seagull at *two hundred fourteen miles per hour!* It was a break-through, the greatest single moment in the history of the Flock, and in that moment a new age opened for Jonathan Gull. Flying out to his lonely practice area, folding his wings for a dive from eight thousand feet, he set himself at once to discover how to turn.

A single wingtip feather, he found, moved a fraction of an inch, gives a smooth sweeping curve at tremendous speed. Before he learned this, however, he found that moving more than one feather at that speed will spin you like a rifle ball . . . and Jonathan had flown the first aerobatics of any seagull on earth.

He spared no time that day for talk with other gulls, but flew on past sunset. He discovered the loop, the slow roll, the point roll, the inverted spin, the gull blunt, the pinwheel.

When Jonathan Seagull joined the Flock on the beach,

it was full night. He was dizzy and terribly tired. Yet in delight he flew a loop to landing, with a snap roll just before touchdown. When they hear of it, he thought, of the Breakthrough, they'll be wild with joy. How much much more there is now to living! Instead of our drab slogging forth and back to the fishing boats, there's a reason to life! We can lift ourselves out of ignorance, we can find ourselves as creatures of excellence and intelligence and skill. We can be free! *We can learn to fly!*

Jonathan Livingston Seagull was first published in 1970. Initially, it was not widely read. But gradually, more and more people discovered it. By 1972, this fable about the hardships and rewards of creativity and individualism had become very popular. The book was #1 on the best seller list for all of 1972 and 1973.

Starting Time		Finishing Time	
Reading Time		Reading Rate	
Comprehension		Vocabulary	

Comprehension— Read the following questions and statements. For each one, put an *x* in the box before the option that contains the most complete or accurate answer. Check your answers in the Answer Key on page 107.

1. The first time Jonathan set a world speed record for seagulls, he flew at
   - ☐ a. 50 miles per hour.
   - ☐ b. 70 miles per hour.
   - ☐ c. 90 miles per hour.
   - ☐ d. 214 miles per hour.

2. Jonathan's parents were upset because he
   - ☐ a. was different from the other gulls.
   - ☐ b. ate too much.
   - ☐ c. refused to obey.
   - ☐ d. caused unrest among the other gulls.

3. Jonathan broke a basic rule of seagull behavior when he
   - ☐ a. began landing on the beach.
   - ☐ b. flew at an altitude of 100 feet.
   - ☐ c. flew at night.
   - ☐ d. flew too close to fishing boats.

4. Jonathan represents the
   - ☐ a. spirit of perfection.
   - ☐ b. fall of man.
   - ☐ c. end of time.
   - ☐ d. quest for glory.

5. Jonathan soon learned that
   - ☐ a. his parents were wiser than he.
   - ☐ b. happiness and pain go together.
   - ☐ c. success and fame are important.
   - ☐ d. the price of perfection is too high.

6. Jonathan's behavior was
   - ☐ a. a common childhood development.
   - ☐ b. a challenge to tradition.
   - ☐ c. a threat to the security of his kind.
   - ☐ d. an amusing development.

7. It can be inferred from the selection that Jonathan will
   - ☐ a. eventually kill himself in an accident.
   - ☐ b. develop into a wild-eyed radical.
   - ☐ c. have problems convincing other seagulls of his skill.
   - ☐ d. become discouraged and return to the flock.

8. Jonathan's mood varied from elation to
   - ☐ a. discouragement.
   - ☐ b. pride.
   - ☐ c. anger.
   - ☐ d. arrogance.

9. Jonathan's father had
   - ☐ a. an unusual flight pattern.
   - ☐ b. a practical turn of mind.
   - ☐ c. a strict and harsh manner.
   - ☐ d. a gentle and quiet manner.

10. Which of the following sentences sets Jonathan Livingston Seagull apart from the other gulls?
    - ☐ a. "It was morning, and the new sun sparkled gold across the ripples of a gentle sea."
    - ☐ b. "But way off alone, out by himself beyond boat and shore, Jonathan Livingston Seagull was practicing."
    - ☐ c. " 'Don't forget that the reason you fly is to eat.' "
    - ☐ d. "I don't mind being bone and feathers, Mom."

Comprehension Skills
1. recalling specific facts	6. making a judgment
2. retaining concepts	7. making an inference
3. organizing facts	8. recognizing tone
4. understanding the main idea	9. understanding characters
5. drawing a conclusion	10. appreciation of literary forms

Study Skills, Part One—Following is a passage with blanks where words have been omitted. Next to the passage are groups of five words, one group for each blank. Complete the passage by selecting the correct word for each of the blanks.

Signs and Signals

In well-written texts you will find many *signs* that are meant to guide the ___(1)___ . Signs are the most obvious guides. They are different from *signals,* which we will discuss later.

For our purposes, signs refer to the use of numbers and letters to point out the value or the sequence of thoughts. Perhaps the most commonly recognized reading signs are the numbers *1, 2, 3,* and so on. Their roles as indicators of worth or order are readily apparent to most readers. Sometimes they are ___(2)___ by another sign: "There are *three* major causes of baldness." Upon seeing the word *three* the reader knows that numbers will soon follow.

Letters are often used in the same way as numbers. *A, B,* and *C* or *a, b,* and *c* ___(3)___ consistently throughout texts to guide the reader.

In addition to numbers and letters, integral words in the text can work as signs. We often see the words *one, two,* and *three,* or *first, second,* and *third.* They have the same ___(4)___ and importance to the reader, even though they do not stand out in the text the way alpha-numeric signs do.

Still other signs are the phrases *in the first place, in the second place,* and so on. They also serve to inform the reader that numbering is taking place, though the reader may be only partially ___(5)___ of that process. But it is essential that such phrases be in some way numbered by the reader if the ideas they list are to have the significance the author intended.

Signs are more likely to appear in certain ___(6)___ in the chapter. Often they are used at the beginning to list the important elements to be covered.

Another place to look for signs is at the end of a chapter or section. There they are used as a summary listing of ___(7)___ elements discussed in the preceding material.

(1)	player		traveler
	reader	writer	driver

(2)	followed		delivered
	inserted	presented	introduced

(3)	sustain		appear
	vanish	count	gain

(4)	value		price
	reason	standard	benefit

(5)	fond		thankful
	approving	grateful	aware

(6)	methods		ways
	places	periods	patterns

(7)	important		unknown
	distinguished	instant	stately

Study Skills, Part Two—Read the study skills passage again, paying special attention to the lesson being taught. Then, without looking back at the passage, complete each sentence below by writing in the missing word or words. Check the Answer Key on page 107 for the answers to Study Skills, Part One, and Study Skills, Part Two.

1. Signs are such _____ guides that we separate them from signals.

2. Signs refer to the use of numbers and _____ to point out important ideas.

3. We may see the word *fourth* used instead of the number _____ .

4. Signs are often found at the _____ of the chapter, listing important things to come.

5. Signs are also found at the end of the chapter where they are used to list _____ of important ideas.

9 | Will the Weather Channel Save America?

by James Gorman

Vocabulary—The five words below are from the story you are about to read. Study the words and their meanings. Then complete the ten sentences that follow, using one of the five words to fill in the blank in each sentence. Mark your answer by writing the letter of the word on the line before the sentence. Check your answers in the Answer Key on page 107.

A. inexorably: unyieldingly; relentlessly

B. succumbed: given in; yielded

C. vouchsafed: granted; bestowed

D. disingenuous: not straightforward; insincere

E. surfeit: excessive amount

_____ 1. Most network television programs have a _____ of action.

_____ 2. Prime time network series are often _____ in their picture of law enforcement.

_____ 3. The author immediately _____ his opinion about sex and death in the same scene.

_____ 4. Plots for *Miami Vice* _____ led to sex and violence.

_____ 5. The Weather Channel has not _____ to the glitzy, action-packed format of other channels.

_____ 6. Fishing is one of the pleasures _____ to those who enjoy a slow-paced activity.

_____ 7. There was nothing _____ about the two men fishing.

_____ 8. Nature shows portray predators _____ hunting down their prey.

_____ 9. The two southern fishermen did not engage in a _____ of conversation.

_____ 10. The author has _____ to the charm and allure of satellite pictures.

I don't want to say flat out that the Weather Channel is the best thing on television. That would leave out the fishing shows. Actually, the fishing shows are the best thing on television. I saw one in which two old southern boys sat in a boat for half an hour without catching anything. That's right, two guys in a boat talking about what it would be like if they did happen to catch something. Zen TV.

On the Weather Channel there's no violence, no car chases, no sex. Just a little rain every now and then.

They weren't unhappy. They just sat there, chatting, flicking their lures out and reeling them in. That was it. That's all that happened. The effect was that slowly, inexorably, the compelling lack of action drew the viewer into the same state of enlightened nothingness that fishermen experience on a slow day on a hot lake. Largemouth bass Nirvana.

Compare this with *Miami Vice,* the television show that introduced to the world the genre of action-couture. In the archetypal *Miami Vice* episode two different scenes were crosscut, or interweaved, much the way tulle and taffeta might be combined in a ballet costume. In one scene thugs were murdering some poor woman. In the other Don Johnson was making love to another poor woman. (My memory is hazy, but I'm sure it wasn't the same woman.) The viewers were heaved back and forth from Don Johnson and his victim to the thugs and their victim until the death of one and the presumptive orgasm of the other occurred simultaneously.

Now I certainly wouldn't want to go around picking on every television show that made me want to throw up. I'd have no time left for fishing. And my complaint about this sex-death bit doesn't have to do with its stomach-turning quality alone. Either scene, on its own, would have made me sick. No, what was sad about this episode was that somebody felt it was necessary to have two nauseating scenes at once. And that's what's wrong with television today—too much stuff happening. On television these days there's no end to the stuff that happens—murders, sex, car chases, wardrobe changes. And now, I suppose, we're going to have to have them all at once.

It's not just the action-couture series either. Television science shows (at least those that deal with subjects other than meteorology) have succumbed to this same undeniable urge to make everything overexciting. Salmon are always spawning, stars are dying and being born, the universe is whirling apart, dinosaurs are going extinct, people are evolving. On the nature shows there is the constant drama of slaughter. (I wonder if the Public Broadcasting System understands how small a role—in terms of protein—the predator-prey relationship plays in the life of the average American.)

You could say this is all just sour grapes on my part because my life is so dull, but you'd be wrong. I change my wardrobe, I have sex—not as much as on *L.A. Law,* but then neither does anybody else—and I was even in a car chase once. It's true. Some lunatic driving a giant bus tried to run me off the Long Island Expressway, all because of a vulgar gesture I happened to have made when he cut in front of me. People are so sensitive.

No, sour grapes is not the ax I have to grind. I like my life. I prefer my clothes to Don Johnson's. And I didn't like being in the car chase at all. I just want TV to reflect my life-style, one which I think is shared by the majority of people in this country. It is a life that consists largely of getting the oil changed in the car and trying to figure out, at the supermarket, whether to buy 80- or 85-percent-lean ground beef. On a big day, I go fishing and don't catch anything.

That's what was so great about the No Fish Fish Show; it was a little bit of actual life that somehow leaked into the television world. It was just like reality. They had only one or two camera angles, which is what we've got in our house. And the show obviously wasn't planned to come out this way. Nobody had edited this film to provide the suspense of fishlessness before the fish finally started to bite. These guys just weren't catching anything. They had gone out in a boat to do their show, and another boat with cameras had followed them, and the people in both boats had spent all day on some stupid lake fishing and talking and filming, and they hadn't caught a damned thing. Then they put this on television.

It was a shock, like when Lex Luthor takes over the television networks in Superman movies. I felt like Winston Smith in *1984.* I had managed to remember who we were at war with. I had remembered that this was what life was actually like—sitting in a boat with no sound track not catching anything. I took the moment as a kind of epiphany vouchsafed to those television viewers with an interest in bass fishing. I had no hopes to see anything like it again. I was satisfied that one such experience was as much as anyone could hope for. But I was wrong. I didn't know, then, about the Weather Channel.

I don't think any of us really expected science to revolutionize television, let alone meteorology. I know I didn't. Like most people I had pinned my hopes on our regional playwrights. In hindsight, now that I've experienced the Weather Channel, I can see why meteorology was such a likely candidate. It has to do with something people understand, for one thing. Rain is a far easier concept to grasp than, say, quantum gravity, or superstrings. You can see rain. You can even see the clouds that make it, in the satellite pictures. Like most Americans I'm a sucker for satellite pictures. This is one reason why there are so few television series on mathematics. No satellite pictures.

Of course, it would be disingenuous of me to suggest that meteorology did it all. A technological breaththrough was also necessary—cable TV. With cable, and with the wide dissemination of remote control for television, people are able to lie on the couch and zip through 20 or 30 or 50 channels and then back again. This makes the surfeit of action on the tube even more obvious. If you do this for a while, you realize very quickly that there's no point in figuring out what show you're watching or what the plot is. All television is made up of interchangeable action modules, and you can switch from car chase to sex to shooting to car chase, never knowing who is chasing or kissing whom, and never caring.

With cable, people watch not shows but the television itself, as if they were looking through a window to check what's going on in the street, or what the weather is. The realization of this fact no doubt inspired the creation of the Weather Channel. Somebody said: Let's forget the whole notion of shows—the viewers have. Let's just have one endless weather forecast that repeats itself over and over. And let's forget about lying to the audience and claiming our channel will be exciting. Let's just claim that if people tune in, we'll tell them about the weather.

The result is something very much like the fishing shows, except that you don't have to like fishing. You don't even have to like the weather that much, because you don't have to watch for very long to find out what's going on. The Weather Channel doesn't really have shows. It has the weather, 24 hours a day, seven days a week, 365 days a year, delivered in bits and pieces, some as short as a minute, some as long as three minutes. You can tune in and tune out anytime you want. There's no violence and no kissing.

During the few weeks that I did my heaviest Weather Channel watching, I admit that there were no hurricanes or deadly tornadoes to throw the channel into frenzy, so my view may be slightly skewed. But this is what I saw: two men, or a man and a woman, with pretty unremarkable haircuts and clothes and looks, not like Diane Sawyer making the rest of us feel dumb and ugly. And they wouldn't talk to you as if something big were happening and you'd better listen up, the way Dan Rather does, because something big wasn't happening.

Mostly they talked about the temperature in different places. They'd tell you the international temperatures—84 in Rome, 92 in Bucharest. And they'd tell you the temperatures in our country and talk about our clouds and our highs and lows and where and when it would rain and snow. One day I learned that it had been 18 in Great Falls the night before and 90 in Miami. It made me think. What a diverse country we live in, I thought, and yet we're all Americans. It was kind of amazing. And when I saw that blue jet stream, done as a kind of video Slinky snaking across the weather map, or looked at the satellite pictures that showed the swirling clouds uniting us all in the movements of the cold fronts and the warm fronts, I felt not only that this channel related to my life—in that the weather they were talking about was the same weather I walked around in—but that I was part of a nationwide weather community. That is the level of excitement I like on my television. And that's the charm of the Weather Channel. In a world of video tarts shaking their goodies all over the screen saying "Hey baby, want to party?" there is one plain, unadorned, mousy little channel that says, "Hi. Some rain, huh?" To me it's irresistible.

Not that it's perfect, yet. We don't really need the maps and the blue snaky jet stream and the suits and ties. And we don't need lots of different weather people. All we really need are two guys, preferably southern, to just sit and chat about the weather. And then, if we could just, well, I know this is asking a lot, but if we could just put them in a boat and let them fish while they talked. Do you see how good that would be? Once in a while they'd catch some fish. It would rain now and then. A little drizzle, nothing big. And they'd talk about the weather. Snow in Colorado, sun in Florida, thunderstorms in Kansas. You could turn to them any time you wanted. Any time of the day or night you could switch to the Fishing and Weather Channel and there they'd be, not Crockett and Tubbs shooting up Miami, but two regular guys, your friends and mine, fishing and talking about the weather.

Starting Time		Finishing Time	
Reading Time		Reading Rate	
Comprehension		Vocabulary	

Comprehension— Read the following questions and statements. For each one, put an *x* in the box before the option that contains the most complete or accurate answer. Check your answers in the Answer Key on page 107.

1. The author claims that *Miami Vice* was the first show presented in the genre of
   - ☐ a. drugs-thugs.
   - ☐ b. sex-death.
   - ☐ c. death-coiffure.
   - ☐ d. action-couture.

2. The Weather Channel offers
   - ☐ a. tips on fishing.
   - ☐ b. a variety of programs.
   - ☐ c. little action.
   - ☐ d. nothing of value.

3. The author discovered the Weather Channel
   - ☐ a. before seeing the No Fish Fish Show.
   - ☐ b. some time after watching the No Fish Fish Show.
   - ☐ c. while watching the No Fish Fish Show.
   - ☐ d. as a result of the No Fish Fish Show.

4. This selection
   - ☐ a. belittles the importance of television.
   - ☐ b. explains the need for television.
   - ☐ c. justifies the use of television.
   - ☐ d. pokes fun at television.

5. The author does not enjoy
   - ☐ a. fishing.
   - ☐ b. nature.
   - ☐ c. adventure programs.
   - ☐ d. weather forecasts.

6. A steady diet of the Weather Channel would be
   - ☐ a. absorbing.
   - ☐ b. educational.
   - ☐ c. entertaining.
   - ☐ d. tiresome.

7. The author believes that *L.A. Law* is
   - ☐ a. unrealistic.
   - ☐ b. too violent.
   - ☐ c. boring.
   - ☐ d. thrilling.

8. The author expects the reader to be
   - ☐ a. amused.
   - ☐ b. amazed.
   - ☐ c. shocked.
   - ☐ d. disappointed.

9. The author prefers to live
   - ☐ a. a reflective, slow-paced life.
   - ☐ b. vicariously through television characters.
   - ☐ c. without any modern conveniences.
   - ☐ d. the rugged life of an outdoorsman.

10. *1984* is a novel written by George Orwell. The sentence, "I felt like Winston Smith in *1984*" contains
   - ☐ a. a literary allusion.
   - ☐ b. a classic understatement.
   - ☐ c. an example of literal language.
   - ☐ d. an attempt at personification.

Comprehension Skills

1. recalling specific facts	6. making a judgment
2. retaining concepts	7. making an inference
3. organizing facts	8. recognizing tone
4. understanding the main idea	9. understanding characters
5. drawing a conclusion	10. appreciation of literary forms

Study Skills, Part One—Following is a passage with blanks where words have been omitted. Next to the passage are groups of five words, one group for each blank. Complete the passage by selecting the correct word for each of the blanks.

Forward Signals

Signals are useful guides for the reader, but they are not as apparent as signs. The first types of signals that we are going to look at are called Forward Signals.

This group of signals tells the reader to ___(1)___ with the

(1)   advance   finish
       endure   insist   end

thought. They indicate that more of the same is coming and that the reader should continue forward.

The most common forward signals are *and, more, moreover, more than that, furthermore, also,* and *likewise.*

The most frequently used word in that group is *and.* It is a forward signal that tells the reader that another item of ___(2)___ importance will follow or that the items are parts of a series. It tells you that you will not be faced with an ___(3)___ or reversing thought—you can go right on for more of the same.

The signals *more, moreover, more than that,* and *furthermore* all indicate that new and even stronger thoughts are coming up: "She's clever all right; *more than that,* she's a genius." It is plain how such signals strengthen and add depth to the ___(4)___ idea.

The signal *likewise* means "in the same manner." *Also,* by the same token, indicates that statements of ideas quite ___(5)___ to those that have preceded are about to follow: "Along with signs, authors *also* use signals." Signals are unlike signs in many ways. Signs, as you recall, stand out in the text; most of them are easy to ___(6)___ . In fact, they are nearly impossible to miss. Signs are usually placed above or in front of the numbered material.

Signals, on the other hand, are words, and they are woven into the text. They are not set apart from the rest of the copy. For that reason, they are not as easy to spot as signs, and they therefore require the reader to be ___(7)___ for their appearance and function.

(2)		rival		equal
	vast		primary	greater

(3)		opposing		easy
	obvious		essential	aggressive

(4)		following		final
	future		previous	different

(5)		different		similar
	advanced		contrasting	simple

(6)		study		refer
	employ		identify	repeat

(7)		present		alert
	eager		restless	absent

Study Skills, Part Two—Read the study skills passage again, paying special attention to the lesson being taught. Then, without looking back at the passage, complete each sentence below by writing in the missing word or words. Check the Answer Key on page 107 for the answers to Study Skills, Part One, and Study Skills, Part Two.

1. Other words that _____ the reader are called signals.

2. Signals are more _____ to find than signs because they do not stand out from the rest of the text.

3. The signals in the first group tell the reader to continue. They are called _____ signals.

4. The signal word *and* is the most common. It joins items of equal importance or items in a _____ .

5. The words *more* and *moreover* are _____ signal words. They tell the reader that the items to follow will add to the original idea.

10 | Henrietta, an Intelligent Fish

by Pauline L. Jensen

Vocabulary—The five words below are from the story you are about to read. Study the words and their meanings. Then complete the ten sentences that follow, using one of the five words to fill in the blank in each sentence. Mark your answer by writing the letter of the word on the line before the sentence. Check your answers in the Answer Key on page 107.

A. adroitly: skillfully; cleverly

B. premonition: forewarning

C. frenzy: wildly excited state

D. wan: unnaturally or unusually pale

E. exasperated: irritated

_____ 1. Martin _____ netted a couple of dozen fish from the fish pool.

_____ 2. People's faces sometimes look _____ in the moonlight.

_____ 3. The author became _____ when she couldn't find Henrietta in the pool.

_____ 4. The author had a _____ that Henrietta and the other fish were in trouble.

_____ 5. At first the narrator seemed _____ by her new pets.

_____ 6. Martin maneuvered the car _____ through the sleet.

_____ 7. The Fosters apparently left their house in a _____ .

_____ 8. After the storm the moon looked _____ .

_____ 9. Some people claim to have a _____ before disaster strikes.

_____ 10. Henrietta went into a _____ of happy activity when she was placed in the pool.

I made a point of saying her name often, even if everyone else thought I'd gone daffy.

Who in the world would ever believe that a woman of my age would flip her cool over a goldfish? Yes, a goldfish!

All my life I had adroitly sidestepped any suggestion of fish as pets. To me, they were the lowest creatures on the totem pole, and that is low.

I had no premonition of what awaited me when I stopped to say good-bye to my friend Laura, who was leaving for a long vacation.

"Come in and sit down," she urged. "I'm ready for a coffee break." She sighed. "I'm weary of packing."

Just as I was leaving, she asked, "Wouldn't you like to have a pair of goldfish?"

"I would *not!*"

"But Henrietta and Silver are such nice fish, and I think they're unusually intelligent."

"No! Not even intelligent fish!"

She frowned. "Well, I guess I'll have to do the inevitable."

"Meaning what?"

"Dump them down the drain."

"You wouldn't."

"I haven't any choice."

Well, that's how we acquired Henrietta and Silver, complete with small tank.

Martin, my husband, gasped as I carried our newest acquisition into the house. "Tell me it isn't so!" He shuddered.

Taking daily care of Henrietta and Silver did nothing to endear them to me. I fed them, changed the water, and wondered how I had ever let myself in for such a task. They came for their food, gulped it down, and resumed their aimless cruising. I tried talking to them, but the only sign of recognition came when I held the fish food over the water.

Then one morning I found Silver floating on top of the water. Since he had eaten heartily the night before, I lifted him and put him in a pan of water to make sure he had departed this life. He had.

Imagination or not, I was sure that Henrietta missed her companion. People talk to their flowers, I thought, so why not try it on Henrietta.

It worked. I began feeding her from my fingers and she would come to the very edge of the tank and remain there until I'd finished my one way conversation before she went back to swimming.

Before long I was convinced she knew her name. With the carton of fish food held aloft, I'd coax her. "Come on, Henrietta, be a good girl and eat your supper." Eat she did, and then she'd flip her tail or fins or both, and stare at me.

"I know now what that old expression 'fish eyes' means," I said to Martin. "Every time I go into the room, she comes zipping over to the front of the tank, begging for attention."

"Maybe for food," Martin said.

"She comes even when I don't have food," I countered. "I think she's lonely, and I'm sure she knows her name."

It got to the point that whenever I went into the room where Henrietta was, I felt guilty because I couldn't give her my whole attention. "After all," I explained, "this dusting has to be done and the vacuum won't operate alone." This explanation brought nothing more than a vigorous tail and fin waving.

Then I had a beautiful idea. I'd get a couple more fish and then Henrietta wouldn't be so lonesome, and my guilty psyche wouldn't be in constant operation.

The next morning as I backed the car out of the garage to go to the pet store, I saw Jane and Tom Foster working in their backyard. I pulled up close to the fence. "What's going on?"

"Come take a look," Jane said. She got up from her knees. "We're going to have a fish pond and it's really terrific." I shut off the car motor and walked over to where Tom was digging a hole about a foot deep. He had outlined it with the hose, and it did look pretty fancy.

"I'm going to put bridges and a couple of caves and a castle in it," he said proudly.

I had a sudden inspiration. "I'll be glad to donate the first customer. In fact, I was just going out to get a couple of companions for Henrietta. How about me picking up a few more fish and donating them, too?" I grinned, "I'd even feed them for the summer."

I knew that would get to Tom's heart. He wasn't known for throwing pennies around.

When the pool was finished, I took Henrietta and the other fish I'd bought and slid them gently into the pool. Henrietta almost went berserk. She darted in and out of the caves, and seemed to be in a frenzy of delight.

Now, I mused as I sauntered back home, Henrietta will really like that pool. Then I had a funny sad feeling. She will forget me, and even forget her name, I'll bet.

Fortunately, I was wrong. Each morning as I fed them, Henrietta was always the first to appear, and the last to leave. I made a point of saying her name often, even if everyone else thought I'd gone daffy.

Henrietta grew fat and sleek. By midsummer a couple dozen tiny golden creatures appeared in the pool. I felt sure Henrietta had contributed her share, and it made me happy.

In late September Martin and I decided to take a vacation. When I left our door key with Jane, I made her promise to bring the fish inside if the weather got bad. "When we get back, I'll take them for the winter," I assured her.

We stayed away longer than we intended. Some business

contacts came up, and Martin had to take care of them. Though the weather was gorgeous, I wondered from time to time how Henrietta fared without my tender loving care.

The day we returned home was miserable. The closer we got, the worse the weather was. Sixty miles from our destination, sleet coated the highway in a solid sheet. Martin drove as carefully as he could, and still skidding, we reached our driveway at a quarter to midnight.

As I passed the dining room with an armload of things, I saw a note on the table. On top of the note were two keys. I had a premonition, for one key was our own, and the other the Fosters'.

Snatching up the note, I read, "Sorry, but we had to leave in a hurry. Tom's mother had a heart attack. I didn't have time to do anything about the fish, but I did leave food so that Debbie, next door, could feed them. Don't worry if they freeze. We can always get more next year. Luv, Jane."

I shivered. Henrietta was out there in the bitter cold and sleet. I handed the note to Martin. "Looks like we have a job to do tonight."

Dressed in warm clothes, and equipped with our battery trouble light, two flashlights, two pails of water, and two sieves, we inched our way to the Fosters'. I reached into my pocket. The carton of fish food I had grabbed at the last minute was still there.

The sleet had stopped, and a wan moon shone palely. The wind from the north was piercing and the temperature could have been that of Alaska.

There was almost an inch of ice covering the pond's surface, except for one open space in the middle. With hands numb from the cold, Martin and I worked until we had cleared the pond of ice. Our actions stirred the fish and they were darting everywhere. I didn't see Henrietta but I reassured myself she'd come pretty soon.

Opposite me, across the pool, Martin grumbled. "How many of those little dinky fish are in here? I think I've snagged a couple of dozen already."

"Planning on fish for breakfast?" a voice behind us asked. Martin jumped to his feet, and I turned so suddenly that I cracked my already aching head against a patio chair. In the feeble light we could see that the speaker was a policeman. We'd been so engrossed in our work we hadn't seen the car come into the alley, nor heard the man approach.

"Would you please tell me what you're doing," the policeman asked. "We had a call about some strange goings-on in this yard, and heard the owners were away."

Patiently Martin explained the situation. "If you want more proof of our identity, we'll wake some of the neighbors. Or you can come to our place and see Mrs. Foster's note. She also left us the key."

"How come with a key you didn't turn on the patio light?"

Martin and I both gasped. "I guess we didn't think of it," Martin answered.

"I still can't find Henrietta," I worried aloud. "All the other adult fish are in the pail except for Henrietta."

I felt the officer's eyes on me. "Henrietta?"

"Henrietta's my pet goldfish. She's very intelligent, and she comes when I call her."

Exasperated and concerned, I put my face down close to the water. "Henrietta, if you don't come, we'll leave you here, and in the morning you'll be wearing a block of ice."

We heard a plop, and out of nowhere came Henrietta. She made a beeline toward me, and swam right into my sieve. I heaved a sigh of relief. "She must have been hiding under one of those rocks and didn't hear me."

The officer cleared his throat.

"Well, I guess that does it," said Martin, getting to his feet.

The officer shook his head. "I wouldn't believe it, but I saw it with my own eyes. That fish came when she talked to it!" He grinned. "There's something fishy about that."

He chuckled at his own pun. Then he grabbed my arm, and a look of suspicion crossed his face.

"Say, you didn't by any chance lure that fish to you by rattling a box of food?" he asked.

This time I chuckled. "I told you that Henrietta is a very intelligent fish."

Starting Time		Finishing Time	
Reading Time		Reading Rate	
Comprehension		Vocabulary	

Comprehension — Read the following questions and statements. For each one, put an *x* in the box before the option that contains the most complete or accurate answer. Check your answers in the Answer Key on page 107.

1. The author's friend Laura was about to
   - ☐ a. go on an extended trip.
   - ☐ b. open her own pet store.
   - ☐ c. visit her ailing father-in-law.
   - ☐ d. build a fish pool.

2. Silver's death was due to
   - ☐ a. overfeeding.
   - ☐ b. unknown causes.
   - ☐ c. neglect.
   - ☐ d. foul water.

3. Henrietta began taking an interest in the author after
   - ☐ a. Silver died.
   - ☐ b. the author spoke to her.
   - ☐ c. the new fish arrived.
   - ☐ d. she was fed.

4. Which of the following concepts does the selection illustrate?
   - ☐ a. Emotional involvement can change a person's attitude.
   - ☐ b. Goldfish make better pets than cats.
   - ☐ c. Neighbors should not get involved in each other's affairs.
   - ☐ d. Husbands and wives should have common interests.

5. Throughout the selection, Martin's attitude toward his wife's interest in goldfish
   - ☐ a. improves considerably.
   - ☐ b. gets progressively worse.
   - ☐ c. does not change.
   - ☐ d. is not known.

6. The line in Jane's note which must have disturbed the author was
   - ☐ a. ". . . we had to leave in a hurry."
   - ☐ b. ". . . I did leave food. . . ."
   - ☐ c. "Don't worry if they freeze."
   - ☐ d. "Luv, Jane."

7. At first, the author did not hide her
   - ☐ a. interest in animals.
   - ☐ b. preference for goldfish.
   - ☐ c. knowledge of pets.
   - ☐ d. dislike of fish.

8. Martin's reaction to Henrietta's attempts at friendliness was
   - ☐ a. sarcastic.   ☐ c. sympathetic.
   - ☐ b. interested.   ☐ d. surprising.

9. Tom, the author's neighbor, seems to be
   - ☐ a. generous to a fault.
   - ☐ b. in poor health.
   - ☐ c. lonely.
   - ☐ d. stingy.

10. The selection abounds in
   - ☐ a. literary references.
   - ☐ b. scientific information.
   - ☐ c. witty dialogue.
   - ☐ d. descriptive detail.

Comprehension Skills

1. recalling specific facts	6. making a judgment
2. retaining concepts	7. making an inference
3. organizing facts	8. recognizing tone
4. understanding the main idea	9. understanding characters
5. drawing a conclusion	10. appreciation of literary forms

Study Skills, Part One—Following is a passage with blanks where words have been omitted. Next to the passage are groups of five words, one group for each blank. Complete the passage by selecting the correct word for each of the blanks.

Summary Signals

We have already seen some signals that appear in the text to encourage the reader to move forward because more ideas of the same kind are coming. As you will recall, they are called Forward Signals.

Other signals that also ____(1)____ the reader forward are called Summary Signals.

They are also Forward Signals, but we put them in their own group because the ____(2)____ they do is much more specific. They signal not only that the thought is going on, but also that a new idea is being introduced. The new idea will be one of summary or consequence.

Words such as *thus, therefore, consequently,* and *accordingly* tell the reader that the author is not only advancing the first thought but is also introducing an added one. That added idea will wrap up what has already been said or will reveal the ____(3)____ of earlier ideas. The

(1)   urge   force
     halt   teach   thrust

(2)   fortune   spot
    job   career   business

(3)   result   reason
    subject   source   origin

reader, alerted by the signal words to the new idea, is made aware that the author has been leading up to a synthesis of the original and new ideas. At that point, the writer will, ideally ___(4)___ and summarize the complete thought and show the result or effect it has caused.

The word *thus* is a Summary Signal. It tells the reader that what follows is not simply more of the same, but is a thought carrying greater ___(5)___ for the reader.

In textbooks especially, Summary Signals ___(6)___ ideas and concepts the author feels are of great importance.

Frequently, Summary Signals appear at the beginning of ___(7)___ that summarize the writer's presentation.

(4)
| | pause | | decrease |
| extend | | minimize | create |

(5)
| | meaning | | expression |
| motion | | enjoyment | involvement |

(6)
| | identify | | ignore |
| include | | contain | discard |

(7)
| | ideas | | questions |
| statements | | reports | opinions |

Study Skills, Part Two—Read the study skills passage again, paying special attention to the lesson being taught. Then, without looking back at the passage, complete each sentence below by writing in the missing word or words. Check the Answer Key on page 107 for the answers to Study Skills, Part One, and Study Skills, Part Two.

1. Summary Signals are a special kind of Forward Signal, because they present the reader with a _____ idea.

2. Summary Signals, therefore, have a job that is more _____ than other Forward Signals.

3. Summary Signals tell the reader that the author has _____ presenting his ideas and is about to state the result or conclusion.

4. In _____ especially, these signals introduce important conclusions by the author.

5. Summary Signals usually appear at the _____ of the author's summary.

11 A Whole Society of Loners and Dreamers

by William Allen

Vocabulary—The five words below are from the story you are about to read. Study the words and their meanings. Then complete the ten sentences that follow, using one of the five words to fill in the blank in each sentence. Mark your answer by writing the letter of the word on the line before the sentence. Check your answers in the Answer Key on page 107.

A. geared: aimed; designed

B. pore: study carefully

C. arduous: difficult; strenuous

D. fortitude: strength of mind; tenacity

E. confirmed: verified; proved

_____ 1. The writing school said that writing was _____ work.

_____ 2. The writing school was _____ to adults.

_____ 3. The author found that accumulating $10 was an _____ task.

_____ 4. The writing school promised that for $10, its editors would _____ over the author's stories.

_____ 5. The author finally concluded that he didn't have the _____ needed to become a writer.

_____ 6. The people who ran the writing school said the author's samples _____ their belief that he had talent.

_____ 7. The author liked to _____ over certain magazine advertisements.

_____ 8. The writing school _____ its courses to unpublished writers.

_____ 9. The author's experience with the writing school _____ his fear that he would never become a writer.

_____ 10. The writing school claimed that writers needed _____ to be successful.

On Sunday afternoons here, if you're tired of taking walks in the country and fighting off the green-bellied hogflies, your next best choice is thumbing magazines at the downtown drugstore. One Sunday not long ago, when I ran out of anything else to thumb, I started looking through one of those magazines geared toward helping new writers achieve success. I used to pore over them a lot when I was a teenager, and the first thing I noticed now was that the ads haven't changed much over the past fifteen years:

"IMAGINE MAKING $5,000 A YEAR WRITING IN YOUR SPARE TIME! Fantastic? Not at all. . . . Hundreds of People Make That Much or More Every Year—and Have Fun Doing It!"

"TO PEOPLE WHO WANT TO WRITE FOR PROFIT BUT CAN'T GET STARTED. Have You Natural Writing Ability? Now a Chance to Test Yourself—FREE!"

"I FIRE WRITERS . . . with enthusiasm for developing God-given talent. You'll 'get fired' too with my 48-lesson home study course. Over-the-shoulder coaching . . . personalized critiques! Amazing sales opportunity the first week. Write for my FREE STARTER KIT."

The ad that struck me the most showed a picture of a handsome and darkly serious young man sitting on a hill, picking his teeth with a weed, and gazing out over the countryside. The caption read: DO YOU HAVE THE "FAULTS" THAT COULD MEAN YOU WERE MEANT TO BE A WRITER? The ad went on to list the outstanding characteristics of writers. They are dreamers, loners, bookworms. They are too impractical, too intense, too idealistic.

When I was fourteen and had just started trying to write, I saw an ad much like this and was overwhelmed by it. That fellow on the hill was just like me, I thought. It was a tremendous feeling to discover that I might not be alone—that there was a whole society of loners and dreamers, that they were called writers, and that by sending off for a free writing IQ test I could find out by return mail if I qualified to climb the hill and chew straw with them.

I took that test and blew the top off it. The writing school said I demonstrated a rare creative potential unlike anything they had seen in years. They did wonder, though, if I had what it took to stick with them through long months of arduous training to develop my raw talent. If I really did have that kind of fortitude, the next step would be to send in some actual samples of my writing.

Spurred, I sent off everything I had ever written—two stories of about 200 words each. One was about some unidentified creatures who lived in dread of an unidentified monster who came around every week or so

The writing school said that I demonstrated a rare creative potential.

to slaughter as many of them as he could. Some of the persecuted creatures had the option of running, hopping, scurrying, or crawling to safety, but the others, for some unexplained reason, couldn't move and had just to stand there and take it. There was a description of the monster's roaring approach. Then the last line hit the reader like a left hook: "The lawn mower ran swiftly over. . . ."

The other story I have preserved these many years:

The Race   Two gleaming hot rods stand side by side, poised and tensed—eager to scream down the hot asphalt track, each secretly confident that he will be the supreme victor. The time is drawing close now; in just a few minutes the race will be on.

There is a last minute check of both cars . . . everything is ready. A yell rings out for everyone to clear the track. The flagman raises the starting flag above his head, pauses for a second, and with a downward thrust of the flag, he sends the cars leaping forward with frightening speed.

They fly down the track, side by side, neither able to take the lead. They are gaining speed with every second. Faster and faster they go, approaching the half-way mark with incredible momentum. . . .

Wait! Something is wrong—one of the cars is going out of control and skidding toward the other car! The rending sound of ripping metal and sliding tires cuts through the air as the two autos collide and spin crazily off the track.

For a moment the tragic panorama is hidden by a self-made curtain of dust, but it isn't a second before the curtain is pulled away by the wind, revealing the horrible sight. There are the two hot rods, one turned over, both broken and smashed. All is quiet. . . .

Two small children, a boy and a girl, get up from the curb where they have been sitting. They eye each other accusingly as they walk slowly across the street where the two broken toy cars lay silent. . . . "Woman driver," grumbles the little boy.   **The End**

The correspondence school's copydesk quickly replied that the writing samples confirmed my aptitude test results and that they looked forward to working with me to the point of publication and beyond. I couldn't imagine what could be beyond publication but finally figured out that they meant to handle my work later as agent-representative. They praised my choice of subject matter, sense of drama, and powerful surprise endings—all of which they said indicated I could sell to the sci-fi market. This made sense, because science fiction was all I had ever read voluntarily except for *Comic Classics* and, as a child,

Uncle Wiggly. The school was particularly impressed by my style, which they said was practically poetry, in places. They made reference to my use of alliteration ("rending sound of ripping metal") and of metaphor ("self-made curtain of dust . . . pulled away by the wind").

They were quick to make clear, however, that what I had here were only germs of stories. They needed to be expanded to publishable lengths and had to have better character development—particularly the one about the bugs and grass being slaughtered by the lawn mower. They said a good writer could give even an insect an interesting personality.

The next step was to send them $10 for each of the two stories—the standard fee for detailed, over-the-shoulder copydesk criticism. Then after these stories had been redone and rushed off for publication, I should enroll in their thirty-six-lesson course, in which I would be taught the ins and outs of plotting, characterization, point of view, theme, tone, and setting. The fee was $10 a lesson, and after my successful completion of the course they would then handle my literary properties, protect my legal rights, etc., for the regular 10 percent.

At this point I began to wonder if I might be going in over my head. I was getting only a dollar a week from my folks and didn't understand half of what the writing school was talking about. In English class I had heard of such terms as "alliteration," "tone," and "point of view" but had no clear idea what they meant. Also I felt like an impostor. I had given my age as twenty-one. Of course, I was strutting because at fourteen I was doing better than anybody they had worked with in years, but I wondered if I could keep it up. "Rending sound of ripping metal" was genius, but could I crank out lines like that on a daily basis? I decided to try.

First I wrote them that I was a little short of cash this month and asked if, just to get started, it would be all right to work on one story for $10 instead of two for $20. They replied that that would be fine—just send in the ten bucks so they could get rolling.

Meanwhile I hadn't been able to get even that much money together. I approached my family and was turned down flat because my father thought there was something unhealthy about people who wanted to write. He was bothered by the school's remark that my writing was like poetry. "If you were a girl, it might be different," he said, and showed me a copy of *Men's Adventure.* "Look here, why don't you get one of these two ninety-eight worm ranches? Or one of these small-game boomerangs?"

After a few days of trying to drum up work around the neighborhood, I realized I wasn't going to be able to pull it off and decided just not to write back. But in a week I got a curt note saying they wanted to help me, were trying to be patient, but I was going to have to be more responsible. They said that writing was 1 percent inspiration and 99 percent perspiration and wondered if in my case the figures might be reversed.

This both goaded and scared me. I wrote back that on account of unexpected medical expenses I could afford to give them only $5 at first. Could they possibly let me have a cut rate? They replied that it was strictly against their policy, but in view of my undeniably vast potential the copydesk team had voted to go along with me just this once—send the $5.

By mowing lawns and selling bottles, I had by this time scraped together $3, but there my earning potential dropped sharply. Another week went by, and I made only 48 cents more. Then a letter arrived stamped in red, front and back: URGENT! IMPORTANT! DO NOT DISCARD! It said I had violated an agreement based on mutual trust and had exactly twenty-four hours to send in the $5. Without exactly spelling it out, they gave the impression that legal action might be taken. The letter ended: "Frankly, Mr. Allen, we're about at our wits' end with you."

I was hurt as well as shaken. I felt that I just didn't have what it takes. If there ever had been a chance of my climbing that hill and sitting with that elite group of loners and dreamers, it was gone now. I had my mother write them that I had suddenly been struck down with polio and was unable even to write my name, much less take their course. I hung onto the little money I had in case I had to give it to them to avoid a lawsuit, but I didn't hear from them after that. In a few weeks I relaxed and mailed off for the $2.98 worm ranch.

Starting Time		Finishing Time	
Reading Time		Reading Rate	
Comprehension		Vocabulary	

Comprehension— Read the following questions and statements. For each one, put an *x* in the box before the option that contains the most complete or accurate answer. Check your answers in the Answer Key on page 107.

1. The author finally asked his mother to
   - ☐ a. loan him $5.
   - ☐ b. write a letter to the school.
   - ☐ c. help him complete a story.
   - ☐ d. buy him a worm ranch.

2. The author feared the school would
   - ☐ a. take legal action against him.
   - ☐ b. close before he completed his course.
   - ☐ c. not accept him into their 36-lesson course.
   - ☐ d. decide he had no talent as a writer.

3. The school refused to provide detailed criticism of the author's story until he
   - ☐ a. sent them some money.
   - ☐ b. offered proof that he was 21 years old.
   - ☐ c. agreed to enroll in a 36-lesson course.
   - ☐ d. demonstrated a real desire to improve his writing skills.

4. The selection is critical of
   - ☐ a. raw talent.
   - ☐ b. young writers.
   - ☐ c. correspondence schools.
   - ☐ d. business schools.

5. The magazine ads were calculated to appeal to the
   - ☐ a. inexperienced.
   - ☐ b. talented.
   - ☐ c. wealthy.
   - ☐ d. educated.

6. The strategy of the correspondence school illustrates which of the following?
   - ☐ a. A satisfied customer always returns.
   - ☐ b. To succeed, one should seem a fool, but be wise.
   - ☐ c. Talent is only a starting point.
   - ☐ d. A sucker is born every minute.

7. The writing school was quick to recognize
   - ☐ a. a person with rare talent.
   - ☐ b. an overtrustful person.
   - ☐ c. an applicant with little potential.
   - ☐ d. a candidate unwilling to work.

8. As time passed, the tone of the letters sent by the writing school changed from
   - ☐ a. doubtful to excited.
   - ☐ b. surprised to disinterested.
   - ☐ c. promising to threatening.
   - ☐ d. cheerful to discouraging.

9. At age fourteen, the author felt that he was
   - ☐ a. an idler and a drifter.
   - ☐ b. a loner and a dreamer.
   - ☐ c. misunderstood.
   - ☐ d. superior.

10. Considering his age, the stories submitted by the writer were
   - ☐ a. good.
   - ☐ b. fantastic.
   - ☐ c. unusual.
   - ☐ d. typical.

Comprehension Skills

1. recalling specific facts	6. making a judgment
2. retaining concepts	7. making an inference
3. organizing facts	8. recognizing tone
4. understanding the main idea	9. understanding characters
5. drawing a conclusion	10. appreciation of literary forms

Study Skills, Part One—Following is a passage with blanks where words have been omitted. Next to the passage are groups of five words, one group for each blank. Complete the passage by selecting the correct word for each of the blanks.

Terminal Signals

We have been looking at two types of signals that urge the reader on, words that indicate the continuance of the same thoughts and ideas.

You will recall that the second type of signal, the Summary Signal, indicates the appearance of an added or more ___(1)___ thought. That new thought, you have

(1)   serious   important
        developed   noteworthy   recent

learned, is brought about as a result or consequence of the previous ideas.

Yet another type of Forward Signal exists. The Terminal Signal, as it is known, plays a critical role in any written matter.

As the label suggests, Terminal Signals tell the reader that the author is   (2)   his remarks. They announce that he has developed all of the thoughts in his presentation, and that he is about to sum them up or   (3)   a conclusion. Some Terminal Signals are *as a result, finally,* and *in conclusion.* They tell the reader that an ongoing thought (which has been nurtured and developed with the aid of Forward Signals) is about to be terminated.

The main   (4)   between Summary and Terminal Signals is that sense of finality. Summary Signals indicate a pause in the forward motion of a thought. The writer uses the pause not only to sum up the original and the added ideas, but also to extend the   (5)   further. He has reached a summary point, but he is not yet ready to state the final conclusion.

Terminal Signals, on the other hand, end the account in an obvious way. Observe the following use of a Terminal Signal:

> Once the police patrols had been doubled and the aid of the occupants enlisted, the cat burglar was caught. *As a result,* this burglar's days of catting are all over.

The phrase *as a result* makes it plain that the author has said all he   (6)   to say on the subject.

As the textbook reader, you can well imagine that the Terminal Signal may present one of the   (7)   points of any chapter or lesson.

(2)		beginning		recording
	creating		concluding	designing

(3)		draw		invent
	guess		reverse	initiate

(4)		distinction		likeness
	connection		agreement	relationship

(5)		subject		division
	lesson		data	reaction

(6)		can		knows
	intends	permits		pretends

(7)		interesting		harmful
	major		minor	trivial

Study Skills, Part Two—Read the study skills passage again, paying special attention to the lesson being taught. Then, without looking back at the passage, complete each sentence below by writing in the missing word or words. Check the Answer Key on page 107 for the answers to Study Skills, Part One, and Study Skills, Part Two.

1. The last Forward Signals to be considered are the _____ Signals.

2. As the name suggests, these signals announce the _____ of the presentation.

3. The ideas following these last statements will be _____ , not more of the same.

4. The main distinction between these signals and Summary Signals is the sense of _____ indicated by Terminal Signals.

5. These signals are important because they mark the completion of the writer's thoughts on the _____ .

12 A Transcendent Moment

by Sheila Solomon Klass

Vocabulary—The five words below are from the story you are about to read. Study the words and their meanings. Then complete the ten sentences that follow, using one of the five words to fill in the blank in each sentence. Mark your answer by writing the letter of the word on the line before the sentence. Check your answers in the Answer Key on page 107.

A. blustery: violently windy

B. brash: hasty; rash and unthinking

C. distraught: extremely anxious

D. coherent: orderly or logical

E. environs: surroundings

_____ 1. The author gave birth to her first baby in foreign _____ .

_____ 2. Perri went into labor on a _____ night.

_____ 3. The author was _____ when she saw her daughter in great pain.

_____ 4. In the end, the author did not regret her _____ decision to brave the storm and travel to Cambridge.

_____ 5. Benjamin was born in the pleasant _____ of the birthing room.

_____ 6. As she traveled to the airport, the author's thoughts were not very _____ .

_____ 7. The author cared more about witnessing the birth of Benjamin than she did about the _____ weather.

_____ 8. The doctor did not seem _____ by the length of Perri's labor.

_____ 9. The author made the _____ decision to crash through the standby line at the People's Express terminal.

_____ 10. Perri was able to carry on a _____ conversation during her labor.

My daughter Perri phoned me late on January 27, 1984, a blustery snowy night. I was half-asleep, having taught five classes that day. "Mom, I'm in labor. Can you come quickly?"

She was in Cambridge, Massachusetts, and I in northern New Jersey. Twenty minutes later, speeding over glassy roads toward Newark Airport through a heavy winter storm, I realized that my answer had been a bit brash—for a 56-year-old, fairly sensible woman. My reasoning, however, was icy clear. My first grandchild could not be born without me. My daughter, though she was 25 and about to become a mother herself, needed her mother there,

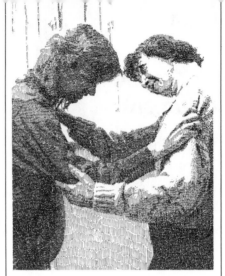

She had borne three children but never seen a baby come into the world until she helped her daughter deliver.

and I needed to be there to help, to make sure everything was all right.

Why wasn't I there to begin with? In the old days, female relatives always rallied 'round at childbirth. Well, in the old days families lived nearer to one another. And women didn't have careers. Perri, a medical student, and Larry, a historian, had planned this baby for the winter break in their academic year. I, too, am on an academic calendar, but my winter recess had ended much earlier.

At the airport an endless line of standbys, skiers in puffy down parkas, slowly boarded the last flight for the night. "Emergency!" I hurried in, shouting, "I have to get on this plane!" and shamelessly, I crashed the line. "She's about to become a grandmother," my husband explained, as if that were a reason.

The airline employees, softened perhaps by my gray hair, his white beard, and our combined distraught behavior, managed to get me aboard, the absolutely last passenger. "Glad to have you with us, Grandma," a portly skier said graciously. "Not Grandma yet," I cautioned, mindful of a lifetime of superstitious warnings.

During all this I hadn't had a single coherent thought. Only sudden rushes. *"The kids" are going to be parents. My child is having a child—extraordinary idea! Why don't we take off? Don't they realize Nature can't wait for People's Express?* I frowned at the steward hoping to impel movement. Across the aisle a woman knitted an argyle sock. *Why didn't I ever learn to knit? What kind of grandmother can't even make booties? I'll learn to knit. I'm going to be a good grandmother. I'm going to be a grandmother!*

Tiredness gone, I was full of energy. I looked to either side of me, but my seatmates were dozing. Lucky for them or they would have heard paeans to incipient grand-motherhood.

During the next hours, my mind's flight outdistanced the plane. I was enchanted by the possibilities: a new life; happiness for Perri and Larry; another person we would love in common; once again, a child to read to—*The Cat in the Hat, Where the Wild Things Are, Charlotte's Web.*

I calculated all the various ways I would be useful: adviser, worrier, shopper, baby-sitter, diagnostician, admirer, teacher. But what came into my head most often was *grandmother.* A remarkable word.

The taxi from Logan Airport screeched along at my urging and got me there just as they were leaving for the hospital. I had made it; now I could guard my daughter so that nothing would go wrong.

Larry, helping Perri, handed me a large cloth bag to carry. It was quite heavy, which surprised me since I knew the plan was to have the baby and go home as soon as possible. Doctors and medical students do not like to be patients in hospitals. This bag seemed loaded for the old-fashioned week-long stay. "Nightclothes, some stuff the childbirth course recommended, and a few odds and ends," Larry said with a grin.

When I got Perri's robe and gown out so she could get ready to be examined, I took inventory. In the bag I found a large bottle of champagne, *Pride and Prejudice* and *Little Women,* a cassette player and tapes they'd made, various soft cloths and a Crockpot to warm the cloths in—they would be used to soothe Perri—potato chips and a jug of apple cider, lingerie and toilet articles, and a small stuffed bear that was an old family member and traveling companion.

Well, they were certainly well prepared. There was even a toy if the baby was precocious.

The doctor's examination determined that Perri was in fine shape, but that it would be a while. We were free to sit in this cheerful birthing room—more a living room than a hospital room with its rocker by the great window overlooking the Charles River—or to wander about in the friendly environs. Nurses would come by to check periodically. Perri should do whatever made her most comfortable.

Walking was what seemed to ease her most. So, through the night we walked, miles and miles up and down corridors and around the birthing room, holding on to one another. When the labor pains became particularly fierce, Perri clutched our shoulders. At intervals, she and Larry breathed in unison as they had practiced. It went on, it seemed to me, endlessly. I tried to encourage her. *Soon,* I began to wish, *soon,* for her sake. As the contractions became more frequent and wrenching, Perri said to me, dazed, "I can't believe you actually did this three times."

Three times, but each time it was over I immediately forgot about labor; the wonder of the new child simply eclipsed the memory. As I had done, so she would too, I knew, but this immediate pain was nonetheless terrible. It was also scary.

The books lay unread, the cassettes unplayed. The soft

cloths cooked in the Crockpot brought some small relief. But during all of this we talked unceasingly, and it was the talk that carried us away from the pain and through the long wait. We talked intermittently of books, of eccentric older relatives; of Perri's brother, who was teaching English in Japan; and particularly of her sister Judy, a high school senior just thinking about college. Should it be a large college or a small one? Gravely, we ticked off the advantages of each. As if we would have any say in her choice.

Perri gasped at me, doubling up. I felt terrible that I had not remembered how bad it could be. "I can't believe you did this three times," she said again.

I began to recount bits of family lore about the first time: Perri's birth in Felicity, a Trinidad village, during an anthropological field trip. Our neighbors, poor East Indians who cut sugar in the cane fields earning a couple of dollars a day, were fascinated that such an old woman as I—30—should be having her *first* baby. They set about helping and protecting me according to local custom. I was not allowed to walk out in the "falling dew" without a head covering; the risk was a stillborn child. I had to eat quantities of okra they provided because it was a slippery vegetable and would promote easy birth. So would having sex frequently, they said, for it kept the passages open. There were a multitude of such rules to be followed. I was carefully supervised.

When my labor pains began, the news ran through Felicity—no phone call needed—and my women friends assembled on our ramshackle porch to lend support. Mistress Bhim, an outspoken protector, assured me, "Don't worry. You no go die." A bit later when I headed for our outhouse, urgently, she barred the way. "Use a 'tensil," she ordered. When I insisted, she came right along with me, determined to make sure this stupid American woman would not lose her baby in the outhouse. How they badgered me, teased me, watched over me. Nobody ever had more support; these Trinidad women were family to me so far away from home.

Frequent and fierce contractions forced Perri to sit down finally in the birthing room. About midday there were signs that this grandchild of mine was about to emerge, but then nothing much happened and more hours passed. With Perri wearying and unable to bear down with sufficient pressure, the doctor suggested that he might have to help the baby out with forceps.

"No!" Perri said, and she began to bear down with renewed energy.

Suddenly, incredibly, it happened. This plump, round, purplish sack appeared. Tiny arms and legs unfolded and there he was, my grandchild, Benjamin!

"How is he?" Perri asked.

"Perfect," I said, for he was.

For me, this was a transcendent moment. Though I had borne three children, I had never actually seen a child come forth. I was always too busy bearing down, breathing, groaning.

The nurse put the baby on Perri's chest so she could see him.

Once Benjamin was here, there was some cleaning up to be done. "There's been a little tearing," the doctor told Perri, apologetically. "I'm going to have to stitch you up."

"Okay," my daughter, the medical student, said. "Would you mind if my mother held the mirror up so I could watch? I'm interested in seeing how it's done."

The doctor was delighted.

So, there I stood holding the mirror carefully angled so she could see, and I watched her studying the doctor stitching away at her vulva. Well, I thought, one thing about children is they never stop surprising you.

What I am really writing about here is love. Benjamin is my constant delight, and I love him dearly. That I was there to support Perri and to witness his beginning was a consecration.

Last time I phoned and got to talk to him, I asked Benjamin the original idiot-grandma question—"How are you?"

"I'm perfect, Grandma," he said, his voice absolutely sunny.

He was and he is.

Starting Time		Finishing Time	
Reading Time		Reading Rate	
Comprehension		Vocabulary	

Comprehension — Read the following questions and statements. For each one, put an *x* in the box before the option that contains the most complete or accurate answer. Check your answers in the Answer Key on page 107.

1. Perri and Larry brought the Crockpot to the hospital to
   - ☐ a. warm up snacks.
   - ☐ b. heat soft cloths.
   - ☐ c. store the champagne.
   - ☐ d. soak Perri's hands in warm water.

2. The author had been invited to Cambridge to
   - ☐ a. witness the birth of Benjamin.
   - ☐ b. care for Benjamin after his birth.
   - ☐ c. comfort Larry during Perri's labor.
   - ☐ d. teach Perri new labor techniques.

3. The author arrived at Perri's house
   - ☐ a. before Perri had gone into labor.
   - ☐ b. too late to be of any real help.
   - ☐ c. in time to help Perri pack her bag.
   - ☐ d. just as Perri was leaving for the hospital.

4. The purpose of the selection is to
   - ☐ a. examine current childbirth practices.
   - ☐ b. warn women about the dangers of giving birth.
   - ☐ c. explain the relationship between the author and her daughter.
   - ☐ d. relate a special event in the life of the author.

5. As a result of her participation in Benjamin's birth, the author felt
   - ☐ a. awkward around Benjamin.
   - ☐ b. especially close to Benjamin.
   - ☐ c. disappointed in Benjamin.
   - ☐ d. responsible for Benjamin.

6. For the author, the birth of her first grandchild was a
   - ☐ a. glorious occasion.
   - ☐ b. painful reminder.
   - ☐ c. bittersweet event.
   - ☐ d. frightening episode.

7. The author's husband
   - ☐ a. supported his wife's decision to travel to Cambridge.
   - ☐ b. resented the author's plan to be present at the birth.
   - ☐ c. wanted nothing to do with Perri and Larry.
   - ☐ d. did not believe in natural childbirth.

8. The selection ends on a
   - ☐ a. humorous note.
   - ☐ b. cautionary note.
   - ☐ c. joyful note.
   - ☐ d. depressing note.

9. The author
   - ☐ a. loves her family very much.
   - ☐ b. gains personal fulfillment from her career.
   - ☐ c. longs to establish closer bonds with her daughter.
   - ☐ d. regrets not having more children.

10. Two examples of alliteration can be found in the selection:
   - ☐ a. "falling dew," purplish sack
   - ☐ b. glassy roads, slippery vegetable
   - ☐ c. bit brash, rallied 'round
   - ☐ d. impel movement, fierce contractions

Comprehension Skills

1. recalling specific facts	6. making a judgment
2. retaining concepts	7. making an inference
3. organizing facts	8. recognizing tone
4. understanding the main idea	9. understanding characters
5. drawing a conclusion	10. appreciation of literary forms

Study Skills, Part One—Following is a passage with blanks where words have been omitted. Next to the passage are groups of five words, one group for each blank. Complete the passage by selecting the correct word for each of the blanks.

Counter Signals

We have been looking mainly at Forward Signals, those signals that tell the reader that a thought is ___(1)___ , that more of the same is coming. We have also discussed Terminal Signals, which are words and phrases the writer uses to tell the reader that an ongoing thought is about to come to an end.

The last signal we will examine does a different job; it signals a reversal of the thought. Called a Counter Signal, this device turns the thought sharply in a different ___(2)___ . It tells the reader to be alert, because a countering idea is soon to appear.

Some common Counter Signals are *but, yet, nevertheless, otherwise, although, despite, in spite of, not, on the contrary,* and *however.* They are all used to introduce an idea not

(1) ending   beginning
     stopping   continuing   developing

(2) direction   station
     form   line   group

only ___(3)___ from what has gone before, but also one that leads the reader in a new direction.

By far the most common Counter Signal is *but*. In the words of English poet Samuel Daniel, "Oh, now comes that bitter word—*but*, which makes all nothing that was ___(4)___ before, that smooths and wounds, that strikes and dashes more than flat denial, or a plain disgrace."

Most of us, like Daniel, can testify to the power of the word. At one time or another we've all overlooked it and suffered the consequences. It is a little word, but it's packed with ___(5)___ . Don't pass over it in your reading— check to see how it affects the sense of the passage.

Indeed, when you come upon any of the Counter Signals, prepare yourself. They tell you that the thought is not going ___(6)___ any longer, that it has stopped. And in textbooks especially, be alert for Counter Signals. They indicate that the author has come to a ___(7)___ in the road and is about to go in a different direction.

(3)	adapted		remaining
	different	continuing	taken

(4)		removed		spent
	traded		separated	said

(5)		joy		significance
	expression		emotion	depression

(6)		forward		backward
	smoothly		slowly	quickly

(7)		man		place
	turn		sign	detour

Study Skills, Part Two—Read the study skills passage again, paying special attention to the lesson being taught. Then, without looking back at the passage, complete each sentence below by writing in the missing word or words. Check the Answer Key on page 107 for the answers to Study Skills, Part One, and Study Skills, Part Two.

1. The final signals to be considered are different from the Forward Signals. They are called _____ Signals.

2. Counter Signals indicate a _____ in thought.

3. Counter Signals not only introduce a different idea, but they also _____ the reader in a new direction.

4. *But* is the most common and probably the most powerful of these words, because it can change the entire _____ of the passage.

5. When you come upon a Counter Signal in a textbook, _____ yourself for a change in direction.

13 | Warm River, I

by Erskine Caldwell

Vocabulary—The five words below are from the story you are about to read. Study the words and their meanings. Then complete the ten sentences that follow, using one of the five words to fill in the blank in each sentence. Mark your answer by writing the letter of the word on the line before the sentence. Check your answers in the Answer Key on page 107.

A. inaudibly: too softly to be heard

B. profile: side view

C. vapor: mist; fog

D. fragments: broken pieces

E. quivering: trembling

_____ 1. The _____ from the river was surprisingly warm.

_____ 2. The author's hands were _____ as he walked up the path to Gretchen's house.

_____ 3. The light from the doorway outlined Gretchen's _____ .

_____ 4. Gretchen's father spoke almost _____ .

_____ 5. Only _____ of Gretchen's past are revealed.

_____ 6. The author sat on the porch, thinking of the river flowing _____ far below him.

_____ 7. At times, Gretchen's father's voice seemed almost to be _____ .

_____ 8. The author was entranced by Gretchen's _____ .

_____ 9. The _____ in the air reminded everyone of the river's constant presence.

_____ 10. _____ of gravel crunched below the feet of the author as he walked toward Gretchen's house.

The driver stopped at the suspended footbridge and pointed out to me the house across the river. I paid him the quarter fare for the ride from the station two miles away and stepped from the car. After he had gone I was alone with the chill night and the star-pointed lights twinkling in the valley and the broad green river flowing warm below me. All around me the mountains rose like black clouds in the night, and only by looking straight heavenward could I see anything of the dim afterglow of sunset.

I wanted to tell her how glad I was to be with her, if only for one night.

The creaking footbridge swayed with the rhythm of my stride and the momentum of its swing soon overcame my pace. Only by walking faster and faster could I cling to the pendulum as it swung in its wide arc over the river. When at last I could see the other side, where the mountain came down abruptly and slid under the warm water, I gripped my handbag tighter and ran with all my might.

Even then, even after my feet had crunched upon the gravel path, I was afraid. I knew that by day I might walk the bridge without fear; but at night, in a strange country, with dark mountains towering all around me and a broad green river flowing beneath me, I could not keep my hands from trembling and my heart from pounding against my chest.

I found the house easily, and laughed at myself for having run from the river. The house was the first one to come upon after leaving the footbridge, and even if I should have missed it, Gretchen would have called me. She was there on the steps of the porch waiting for me. When I heard her familiar voice calling my name, I was ashamed of myself for having been frightened by the mountains and the broad river flowing below.

She ran down the gravel path to meet me.

"Did the footbridge frighten you, Richard?" she asked excitedly, holding my arm with both of her hands and guiding me up the path to the house.

"I think it did, Gretchen," I said; "but I hope I outran it."

"Everyone tries to do that at first, but after going over it once, it's like walking a tightrope. I used to walk tightropes when I was small—didn't you do that, too, Richard? We had a rope stretched across the floor of our barn to practice on."

"I did, too, but it's been so long ago I've forgotten how to do it now."

We reached the steps and went up to the porch. Gretchen took me to the door. Someone inside the house was bringing a lamp into the hall, and with the coming of the light I saw Gretchen's two sisters standing just inside the open door.

"This is my little sister, Anne," Gretchen said. "And this is Mary."

I spoke to them in the semidarkness, and we went on into the hall. Gretchen's father was standing beside a table holding the lamp a little to one side so that he could see my face. I had not met him before.

"This is my father," Gretchen said. "He was afraid you wouldn't be able to find our house in the dark."

"I wanted to bring a light down to the bridge and meet you, but Gretchen said you would get here without any trouble. Did you get lost? I could have brought a lantern down with no trouble at all."

I shook hands with him and told him how easily I found the place.

"The hack driver pointed out to me the house from the other side of the river, and I never once took my eyes from the light. If I had lost sight of the light, I'd probably be stumbling around somewhere now in the dark down there getting ready to fall into the water."

He laughed at me for being afraid of the river.

"You wouldn't have minded it. The river is warm. Even in winter, when there is ice and snow underfoot, the river is as warm as a comfortable room. All of us here love the water down there."

"No, Richard, you wouldn't have fallen in," Gretchen said, laying her hand in mine. "I saw you the moment you got out of the hack, and if you had gone a step in the wrong direction, I was ready to run to you."

I wished to thank Gretchen for saying that, but already she was going to the stairs to the floor above, and calling me. I went with her, lifting my handbag in front of me. There was a shaded lamp, lighted but turned low, on the table at the end of the upper hall, and she picked it up and went ahead into one of the front rooms.

We stood for a moment looking at each other, and silent.

"There is fresh water in the pitcher, Richard. If there is anything else you would like to have, please tell me. I tried not to overlook anything."

"Don't worry, Gretchen," I told her. "I couldn't wish for anything more. It's enough just to be here with you, anyway. There's nothing else I care for."

She looked at me quickly, and then she lowered her eyes. We stood silently for several minutes, while neither of us could think of anything to say. I wanted to tell her how glad I was to be with her, even if it was only for one night, but I knew I could say that to her later. Gretchen knew why I had come.

"I'll leave the lamp for you, Richard, and I'll wait downstairs for you on the porch. Come as soon as you are ready."

She had left before I could offer to carry the light to the stairhead for her to see the way down. By the time I had picked up the lamp, she was out of sight down the stairs.

I walked back into the room and closed the door and bathed my face and hands, scrubbing the train dust with brush and soap. There was a row of hand-embroidered towels on the rack, and I took one and dried my face and hands. After that I combed my hair, and I found a fresh handkerchief in the handbag. Then I opened the door and went downstairs to find Gretchen.

Her father was on the porch with her. When I walked through the doorway, he got up and gave me a chair between them. Gretchen pulled her chair closer to mine, touching my arm with her hand.

"Is this the first time you have been up here in the mountains, Richard?" her father asked me, turning in his chair toward me.

"I've never been within a hundred miles of here before, sir. It's a different country up here, but I suppose you would think the same about the coast, wouldn't you?"

"Oh, but Father used to live in Norfolk," Gretchen said. "Didn't you, Father?"

"I lived there for nearly three years."

There was something else he would say, and both of us waited for him to continue.

"Father is a master mechanic," Gretchen whispered to me. "He works in the railroad shops."

"Yes," he said after a while. "I've lived in many places, but here is where I wish to stay."

My first thought was to ask him why he preferred the mountains to other sections, but suddenly I was aware that both he and Gretchen were strangely silent. Between them, I sat wondering about it.

After a while he spoke again, not to me and not to Gretchen, but as though he were speaking to someone else on the porch, a fourth person whom I had failed to see in the darkness. I waited, tense and excited, for him to continue.

Gretchen moved her chair a few inches closer to mine, her motions gentle and without sound. The warmth of the river came up and covered us like a blanket on a chill night.

"After Gretchen and the other two girls lost their mother," he said, almost inaudibly, bending forward over his knees and gazing out across the broad green river, "after we lost their mother, I came back to the mountains to live. I couldn't stay in Norfolk, and I couldn't stand it in Baltimore. This was the only place on earth where I could find peace. Gretchen remembers her mother, but neither of you can yet understand how it is with me. Her mother and I were born here in the mountains, and we lived here together for almost twenty years. Then after she left us, I moved away, foolishly believing that I could forget. But I was wrong. Of course I was wrong. A man can't forget the mother of his children, even though he knows he will never see her again."

Gretchen leaned closer to me, and I could not keep my eyes from her darkly framed profile beside me. The river below us made no sound, but the warmth of its vapor would not let me forget that it was still there.

Her father had bent farther forward in his chair until his arms were resting on his knees, and he seemed to be trying to see someone on the other side of the river, high on the mountaintop above it. His eyes strained, and the shaft of light that came through the open doorway fell upon them and glistened there. Tears fell from his face like fragments of stars, burning into his quivering hands until they were out of sight.

Presently, still in silence, he got up and moved through the doorway. His huge shadow fell upon Gretchen and me as he stood there momentarily before going inside. I turned and looked toward him but, even though he was passing from sight, I could not keep my eyes upon him.

Gretchen leaned closer against me, squeezing her fingers into the hollow of my hand and touching my shoulder with her cheeks as though she were trying to wipe something from them. Her father's footsteps grew fainter, and at last we could not longer hear him.

Best known for the sensationalism of his novels about rural Southern life, American author Erskine Caldwell wrote more than 40 books, the most famous of them portraying the changing cultural and economic conditions of poor white tenant farmers. Born in White Oak, Georgia, in 1903, Caldwell first became famous in 1932 with his novel *Tobacco Road*. It was later adapted into a play that ran for more than seven years on Broadway.

Starting Time		Finishing Time	
Reading Time		Reading Rate	
Comprehension		Vocabulary	

Comprehension — Read the following questions and statements. For each one, put an *x* in the box before the option that contains the most complete or accurate answer. Check your answers in the Answer Key on page 107.

1. The author had traveled to the footbridge
   - ☐ a. in a taxi.
   - ☐ b. with a group of friends.
   - ☐ c. on a bicycle.
   - ☐ d. with Gretchen.

2. After reaching the house, Richard realized that
   - ☐ a. his fears had been justified.
   - ☐ b. he was angry with himself.
   - ☐ c. he should not have been frightened.
   - ☐ d. his friends had been worried.

3. Richard met Gretchen's father for the first time
 □ a. when he moved to Norfolk.
 □ b. before leaving Baltimore.
 □ c. the night he visited Gretchen's house.
 □ d. after marrying Gretchen.

4. Richard came to the river to
 □ a. see Gretchen.
 □ b. take a swim.
 □ c. talk to Gretchen's father.
 □ d. study the temperature of the water.

5. Gretchen
 □ a. resented her life in the mountains.
 □ b. understood her father's strange silence.
 □ c. neglected to plan for Richard's safety.
 □ d. hid the truth about her father.

6. Gretchen's father found the mountains
 □ a. comforting.
 □ b. unnerving.
 □ c. boring.
 □ d. exciting.

7. The fare Richard paid from the station to the footbridge suggests
 □ a. runaway inflation.
 □ b. a short drive.
 □ c. an earlier time.
 □ d. poor transportation.

8. The atmosphere of the selection is
 □ a. evil.
 □ b. quietly haunting.
 □ c. passionate.
 □ d. comfortably secure.

9. Gretchen's father was
 □ a. lonely.
 □ b. stingy.
 □ c. unfriendly.
 □ d. bitter.

10. The semidarkness
 □ a. conceals the poverty of Gretchen's home.
 □ b. intensifies the mood of the story.
 □ c. enables the characters to hide their feelings about each other.
 □ d. interferes with Richard's purpose.

Comprehension Skills

1. recalling specific facts	6. making a judgment
2. retaining concepts	7. making an inference
3. organizing facts	8. recognizing tone
4. understanding the main idea	9. understanding characters
5. drawing a conclusion	10. appreciation of literary forms

Study Skills, Part One—Following is a passage with blanks where words have been omitted. Next to the passage are groups of five words, one group for each blank. Complete the passage by selecting the correct word for each of the blanks.

Mastering the Text, I

According to the old saying, a workman is only as good as his tools. That is, of course, if he knows how to use them. But what about students? Their tools of learning are textbooks, and the quality of their work depends in large measure on how ___(1)___ they use them.

Fortunately, most modern textbooks are well organized. Publishers try to be sure that their texts are up-to-date, broad in scope, and direct. Because texts are so well ___(2)___ , students can take advantage of those very features.

EVALUATE THE AUTHOR

Naturally, the author knows more about the ___(3)___ than you do; you cannot judge him on that basis. But you can try to learn about his background and experience.

(1)	poorly	well
quickly	often	generously

(2)	known	used
oiled	constructed	appreciated

(3)	subject	history
sincerity	intentions	associations

Is he a lecturer or professor? If so, where does he teach? In addition to teaching, does the writer work in the field? That information may tell you whether his ___(4)___ is theoretical or practical. The level at which he teaches may tell you how general or detailed his writing will be.

In looking for such background information, it is helpful to read the author's preface or introduction. There you will learn if he regards his text as an intensive discussion or a broad survey. You may also find out if he plans to draw on his experiences in the field. Most importantly, you can avail yourself of the chance to examine the author's ___(5)___ for writing the book. You will learn what is expected of you, and why the author considers the subject useful and necessary. Any ideas for you to keep in mind as you use the text should be covered in the preface. Such ___(6)___ remarks are designed to get you off to a good start.

In addition, you should check the copyright date to make sure that the book is current. In today's world, new ___(7)___ accumulates hourly. Therefore it is essential that textbook material is timely enough to be of use.

(4)	background	approach
	emotion	politics	contacts

(5)	salary	reason
	opening	talent	preparation

(6)	closing	exciting
	opening	interesting	formal

(7)	study	information
	machinery	chemistry	experimentation

Study Skills, Part Two—Read the study skills passage again, paying special attention to the lesson being taught. Then, without looking back at the passage, complete each sentence below by writing in the missing word or words. Check the Answer Key on page 107 for the answers to Study Skills, Part One, and Study Skills, Part Two.

1. A good mechanic must know how to _____ his tools.

2. Publishers make an effort to produce _____ textbooks.

3. It is possible for the student to _____ about the author's

    background and experience.

4. Working in the field gives the author a _____ approach to

    the subject.

5. The first opportunity for the author to address the reader is offered by

    the _____ .

14 | Warm River, II

by Erskine Caldwell

Vocabulary—The five words below are from the story you are about to read. Study the words and their meanings. Then complete the ten sentences that follow, using one of the five words to fill in the blank in each sentence. Mark your answer by writing the letter of the word on the line before the sentence. Check your answers in the Answer Key on page 108.

A. mingled: mixed

B. expanding: increasing in size

C. muffled: dulled or deadened sound

D. shaft: ray or beam

E. revelation: sudden discovery

_____ 1. Gretchen's footsteps were _____ by the closed door.

_____ 2. Richard was stunned by the _____ that men could love women with the same intensity as women loved men.

_____ 3. Each light from the valley sent a _____ of light out through the darkness.

_____ 4. As Richard watched Gretchen kneeling by her bed, he felt his feelings for her _____ .

_____ 5. From his room, Richard heard the _____ sounds of Gretchen moving about.

_____ 6. Smoke from Richard's cigarettes _____ with the fresh air out of the mountains.

_____ 7. When Richard opened Gretchen's door, a _____ of light fell across the floor.

_____ 8. The noise from the train _____ with the other sounds in the night air.

_____ 9. Gretchen must have been surprised by the _____ that Richard did indeed love her.

_____ 10. Richard's _____ interest in the river may have caught Gretchen off guard.

Somewhere below us, along the bank of the river, an express train crashed down the valley, creaking and screaming through the night. Occasionally its lights flashed through the openings in the darkness, dancing on the broad green river like polar lights in the north, and the metallic echo of its steel rumbled against the high walls of the mountains.

Gretchen clasped her hands tightly over my hand, trembling to her finger tips.

"Richard, why did you come to see me?"

Her voice was mingled with the screaming metallic echo of the train that now seemed far off.

"I'm not going back this morning—I don't know what was the matter with me last night."

I had expected to find her looking up into my face, but when I turned to her, I saw that she was gazing far down into the valley, down into the warm waters of the river. She knew why I had come, but she did not wish to hear me say why I had.

I did not know why I had come to see her, now. I had liked Gretchen, and I had desired her above anyone else I knew. But I could not tell her that I loved her, after having heard her father speak of love. I was sorry I had come, now after having heard him speak of Gretchen's mother as he did. I knew Gretchen would give herself to me, because she loved me; but I had nothing to give her in return. She was beautiful, very beautiful, and I had desired her. That was before. Now, I knew that I could never again think of her as I had come prepared.

"Why did you come, Richard?"

"Why?"

"Yes, Richard; why?"

My eyes closed, and what I felt was the memory of the star-pointed lights twinkling down in the valley and the warmth of the river flowing below the caress of her fingers as she touched my arm.

"Richard, please tell me why you came."

"I don't know why I came, Gretchen."

"If you only loved me as I love you, Richard, you would know why."

Her fingers trembled in my hand. I knew she loved me. There had been no doubt in my mind from the first. Gretchen loved me.

"Perhaps I should not have come," I said. "I made a mistake, Gretchen. I should have stayed away."

"But you will be here only for tonight, Richard. You are leaving early in the morning. You aren't sorry that you came for just this short time, are you, Richard?"

"I'm not sorry that I am here, Gretchen, but I should not have come. I didn't know what I was doing. I haven't any right to come here. People who love each other are the only ones—"

"But you do love me just a little, don't you, Richard?

You couldn't possibly love me nearly so much as I love you, but can't you tell me that you do love me just a little? I'll feel much happier after you have gone, Richard."

"I don't know," I said, trembling.

"Richard, please—"

With her hands in mine I held her tightly. Suddenly I felt something coming over me, a thing that stabbed my body with its quickness. It was as if the words her father had uttered were becoming clear to me. I had not realized before that there was such a love as he had spoken of. I had believed that men never loved women in the same way that a woman loved a man, but now I knew there could be no difference.

We sat silently, holding each other's hands for a long time. It was long past midnight, because the lights in the valley below were being turned out; but time did not matter.

Gretchen clung softly to me, looking up into my face and laying her cheek against my shoulder. She was as much mine as a woman ever belongs to a man, but I knew then that I could never force myself to take advantage of her love, and to go away knowing that I had not loved her as she loved me. I had not believed any such thing when I came. I had traveled all that distance to hold her in my arms for a few hours, and then to forget her, perhaps forever.

When it was time for us to go into the house, I got up and put my arms around her. She trembled when I touched her, but she clung to me as tightly as I held her, and the hammering of her heart drove into me, stroke after stroke, like an expanding wedge, the spears of her breasts.

"Richard, kiss me before you go," she said.

She ran to the door, holding it open for me. She picked up the lamp from the table and walked ahead to the stairs to the floor above.

At my door she waited until I could light her lamp, and then she handed me mine.

"Good night, Gretchen," I said.

"Good night, Richard."

I turned down the wick of her lamp to keep it from smoking, and then she went across the hall toward her room.

"I'll call you in the morning in time for you to catch your train, Richard."

"All right, Gretchen. Don't let me oversleep, because it leaves the station at seven-thirty."

"I'll wake you in plenty of time, Richard," she said.

The door was closed after her, and I turned and went into my room. I shut the door and slowly began to undress. After I had blown out the lamp and had got into bed, I lay tensely awake. I knew I could never go to sleep, and

I sat up in bed and smoked cigarette after cigarette, blowing the smoke through the screen of the window. The house was quiet. Occasionally, I thought I heard the sounds of muffled movements in Gretchen's room across the hall, but I was not certain.

I could not determine how long a time I had sat there on the edge of the bed, stiff and erect, thinking of Gretchen, when suddenly I found myself jumping to my feet. I opened the door and ran across the hall. Gretchen's door was closed, but I knew it would not be locked, and I turned the knob noiselessly. A slender shaft of light broke through the opening I had made. It was not necessary to open the door wider, because I saw Gretchen only a few steps away, almost within arm's reach of me. I closed my eyes lightly for a moment, thinking of her as I had all during the day's ride up from the coast.

Gretchen had not heard me open the door, and she did not know I was there. Her lamp was burning brightly on the table.

I had expected to find her awake, and I had thought surely she would be in bed. She knelt on the rug beside her bed, her head bowed over her arms and her body shaken with sobs.

Gretchen's hair was lying over her shoulders, tied over the top of her head with a pale blue ribbon. Her nightgown was white silk, hemmed with a delicate lace, and around her neck the collar of lace was thrown open.

I knew how beautiful she was when I saw her then, even though I had always thought her lovely. I had never seen a girl so beautiful as Gretchen.

She had not heard me at her door, and she still did not know I was there. She knelt beside her bed, her hands clenched before her, crying.

When I had first opened the door, I did not know what I was about to do, but now that I had seen her in her room, kneeling in prayer beside her bed, unaware that I was looking upon her and hearing her words and sobs, I was certain that I could never care for anyone else as I did for her. I had not known until then, but in the revelation of a few seconds I knew that I did love her.

I closed the door softly and went back to my room. There I found a chair and placed it beside the window to wait for the coming of day. At the window I sat and looked down into the bottom of the valley where the warm river lay. As my eyes grew more accustomed to the darkness, I felt as if I were coming closer and closer to it, so close that I might have reached out and touched the warm water with my hands.

Later in the night, toward morning, I thought I heard someone in Gretchen's room moving softly over the floor as one who would go from window to window. Once I was certain I heard someone in the hall, close to my door.

When the sun rose over the top of the mountain, I got up and dressed. Later, I heard Gretchen leave her room and go downstairs. I knew she was hurrying to prepare breakfast for me before I left to get on the train. I waited a while, and after a quarter of an hour I heard her coming back up the stairs. She knocked softly on my door, calling my name several times.

I jerked open the door and faced her. She was so surprised at seeing me there, when she had expected to find me still asleep, that she could not say anything for a moment.

"Gretchen," I said, grasping her hands, "don't hurry to get me off—I'm not going back this morning—I don't know what was the matter with me last night—I know now that I love you—"

"But, Richard—last night you said—"

"I did say last night that I was going back early this morning, Gretchen, but I didn't know what I was talking about. I'm not going back now until you go with me. I'll tell you what I mean as soon as breakfast is over. But first of all I wish you would show me how to get down to the river. I have got to go down there right away and feel the water with my hands."

Starting Time		*Finishing Time*	
Reading Time		*Reading Rate*	
Comprehension		*Vocabulary*	

Comprehension— Read the following questions and statements. For each one, put an *x* in the box before the option that contains the most complete or accurate answer. Check your answers in the Answer Key on page 108.

1. Richard planned to leave by
   - ☐ a. car.
   - ☐ b. train.
   - ☐ c. foot.
   - ☐ d. plane.

2. Gretchen was
   - ☐ a. deeply in love with Richard.
   - ☐ b. hurt by her father's attitude.
   - ☐ c. afraid of the river.
   - ☐ d. in a hurry for Richard to leave.

3. Richard realized that he loved Gretchen
   - ☐ a. the moment he arrived at her house.
   - ☐ b. only when it was time for him to leave.
   - ☐ c. when he saw her praying and sobbing.
   - ☐ d. as he listened to Gretchen's father speak.

4. If Gretchen knew why Richard had come, why did she keep asking him to explain?
   - ☐ a. She wanted him to love her.
   - ☐ b. She wanted him to leave.
   - ☐ c. She wanted him to stay.
   - ☐ d. She knew her father was listening.

5. Who, unknowingly, plays a key role in the outcome of the story?
   - ☐ a. Richard
   - ☐ b. Gretchen
   - ☐ c. Gretchen's father
   - ☐ d. Anne and Mary

6. As the story progresses, Richard's attitude goes from
   - ☐ a. patient to impatient.
   - ☐ b. amused to disillusioned.
   - ☐ c. indifferent to resentful.
   - ☐ d. casual to serious.

7. Gretchen's mother and father had been
   - ☐ a. tireless travelers.
   - ☐ b. happily married.
   - ☐ c. unusually strict.
   - ☐ d. very poor.

8. In the evening, Gretchen speaks to Richard
   - ☐ a. despondently.
   - ☐ b. pleadingly.
   - ☐ c. harshly.
   - ☐ d. nervously.

9. Gretchen is many things, but she is especially
   - ☐ a. prudent.
   - ☐ b. talented.
   - ☐ c. friendly.
   - ☐ d. trusting.

10. The river was a symbol of
   - ☐ a. comfort.
   - ☐ b. death.
   - ☐ c. sorrow.
   - ☐ d. fear.

Comprehension Skills

1. recalling specific facts	6. making a judgment
2. retaining concepts	7. making an inference
3. organizing facts	8. recognizing tone
4. understanding the main idea	9. understanding characters
5. drawing a conclusion	10. appreciation of literary forms

Study Skills, Part One—Following is a passage with blanks where words have been omitted. Next to the passage are groups of five words, one group for each blank. Complete the passage by selecting the correct word for each of the blanks.

Mastering the Text, II

After checking on the author, it will be of help to look at two of the standard features of a textbook, the Table of Contents and the Bibliography.

Table of Contents. Next to the chapters themselves, this is the most important part of the ___(1)___ . It shows not only the material covered, but also how the material is organized. If the subject is dealt with historically, from its beginnings to the present, you know that the most current material will come at the end.

The author's approach may not be historical. For instance, if it is an analytic approach, the simple, basic ideas will be discussed ___(2)___ in the text. You will need to know and understand those if you are to grasp complex material presented later.

In examining the table of contents you can tell how the subject will be ___(3)___ , even if you are not well versed in it. You may see listed in the table of contents a section

(1) text   lesson
     chapter   bibliography   features

(2) late   thoroughly
     early   briefly   thoughtfully

(3) determined   learned
     understood   presented   decided

that interests you. Prereading that section will add to your ___(4)___ in the subject area and may help you appreciate the rest of the material in the text.

The Bibliography. At the end of a book you will find the bibliography, which is a list of other books that were used by the author as ___(5)___ or source materials. That list can be a good indication of how the author put the book together. For instance, by reading the publishing dates of the books listed, you can see if the author used both early and ___(6)___ books on the subject. By examining the level of the sources you can judge if they are comprehensive or highly specialized. Perhaps you will even see a book cited that you will want to read for ___(7)___ information.

(4) assistance background situation character analysis

(5) reference dictionary glossary aids biography

(6) historical current fiction famous unauthorized

(7) additional interesting assigned neglected basic

Study Skills, Part Two—Read the study skills passage again, paying special attention to the lesson being taught. Then, without looking back at the passage, complete each sentence below by writing in the missing word or words. Check the Answer Key on page 108 for the answers to Study Skills, Part One, and Study Skills, Part Two.

1. The table of contents reveals the material covered in the book and how it is _____ .

2. _____ presentation proceeds from the earliest to the latest.

3. Analytical presentation proceeds from the simple to the _____ .

4. After looking at the table of contents, you may wish to _____ a section that sounds interesting.

5. The bibliography is a list of books used by the author to obtain _____ on his subject.

15 | **Organ Hunter**

by Andrew C. Revkin

Vocabulary—The five words below are from the story you are about to read. Study the words and their meanings. Then complete the ten sentences that follow, using one of the five words to fill in the blank in each sentence. Mark your answer by writing the letter of the word on the line before the sentence. Check your answers in the Answer Key on page 108.

A. ideal: perfect

B. collaborated: worked together

C. deprived: denied; taken away

D. absorb: accept the impact of

E. tack: approach

_____ 1. Cantirino has _____ with doctors and hospitals throughout New York City.

_____ 2. Cantirino uses a gentle _____ in dealing with families of potential organ donors.

_____ 3. Dialysis patients are _____ of a normal life.

_____ 4. It is not always easy for people to _____ the information that Cantirino has to give them.

_____ 5. In many ways, Cantirino is the _____ organ hunter.

_____ 6. The _____ that Cantirino takes with families of potential donors is not always successful.

_____ 7. The shock of their son's death was hard for the family to _____ .

_____ 8. If a person is _____ of oxygen for an extended period of time, he or she will die.

_____ 9. There is no _____ way to tell a family that their son is brain dead.

_____ 10. Many doctors who have dealt with brain dead accident victims have _____ with Cantirino.

Bill Cantirino is home in Brooklyn on a Tuesday night, relaxing after dinner, when a shrill beeping sound tells him there is work to be done. He turns off the electronic page on his belt and is soon on the phone with a doctor at nearby Maimonides Medical Center. The doctor says they have a man in intensive care who looks ideal. He was carried into the emergency room the night before with a bullet in his neck.

Two policemen said the man had tried to gun them down after they pulled over the stolen Cadillac he was driving. They had both opened fire. The bullet cut a carotid artery, one of the main sources of blood to the brain. A surgeon worked for five hours trying to piece together the torn artery while others tried to keep the man alive. They finally stabilized him, but they were too late. His body was being kept alive on a variety of machines, but his brain had died.

Cantirino gets the name of the man's family and says he'll be in the next day. He thanks the doctor and hangs up the phone.

For Cantirino, tragedy means business. In an average week he has two or three such conversations. As one of two organ hunters for the Gift of Life Organ Procurement Organization, he is on 24-hour call, waiting to get word of potential organ donors.

The nonprofit Brooklyn-based group, part of a growing nationwide organ-sharing network, seeks hearts, livers, corneas, even skin. But its stock-in-trade is kidneys: 8,976 kidney transplants were performed in this country in 1986. There were another 10,000 people with kidney failure on waiting lists for transplants.

"It costs more than thirty thousand dollars a year to keep somone on an artifical kidney," Cantirino says. "A transplant for the first year costs forty-five or fifty thousand. But the second year's cost drops to five thousand, and it goes down from there as dosages of antirejection drugs drop and office visits become less frequent. In terms of money alone, who could question the need for more transplants?"

The problem is that the demand for organs now far exceeds the supply. Patients waiting for transplants of vital body parts must wait for an anonymous death and for people like Cantirino to go to work. His job calls for him first to locate a special kind of death—a death in which the brain is completely destroyed but the body hangs in a sort of limbo, sustained with machines and drugs but never able to be resurrected as a living person. Such deaths are usually caused by physical trauma to the head or lack of oxygen.

Deaths that make for good organ donors are therefore usually of the unexpected kind—the result of car accidents, shootings, or suicides. Once he has located such a case,

Somehow he must find a way to ask this grieving family to make one last sacrifice.

Cantirino must try to convince parents or children or spouses in the depths of grief to donate organs from the deceased. Cantirino has to be a diplomat and psychologist, social worker and undertaker, rolled into one. He is often asked why he does such a thing. And his reply is always the same: "Because I was once given a second chance." Twelve years ago a kidney transplant saved his life.

On Wednesday morning Cantirino calls the family of the shooting victim and arranges to meet them at the hospital that afternoon. He says he usually tries to talk with the whole family, even though he needs the consent of only the next of kin. "They all have to live with this later on," he says.

He drives to Maimonides hospital early, to get a look at the prospective donor and to talk things over with the hospital staff. As he weaves his Oldsmobile around the potholes and broken bottles that pock Fort Hamilton Parkway, he says he can afford to give this family a few days to make up their mind. "As much as I would want the kidneys tonight, I would never press the family," Cantirino says. "I would never make it a point of saying, 'Look, if we don't get them now, it's too late.' I would rather lose them and walk away."

In the small intensive care unit of the fourth floor of Maimonides hospital, Cantirino meets with the young doctor who called him the night before. They had collaborated several weeks earlier on another donation. A 19-year-old boy had been shot while trying to hold up a store. The doctor called Cantirino, and after three days of talks with the family, they got the consent. Cantirino says he has developed personal contacts in emergency rooms and intensive care units throughout New York City; it helps speed up the search. He brings the doctor up-to-date on the previous case: the recipients of both kidneys are doing fine.

Their attention now turns to the prospective donor. The doctor produces a blue folder labeled "Patient Record Number Eight." Canitirino thumbs through page after page of scribbled entries—blood pressure, heart rate, doses of dopamine and other drugs, electrocardiograms, and electro-encephalograms. "Looks good," he grunts. "Good donor."

A nurse tells Cantirino that the family is out in the hall—a few cousins and uncles, the victim's parents, and his sisters. "Most of our cases are either gunshot wounds or auto accidents," Cantirino says. "This is typical of how you have to deal with a family, because there's a guy who all of a sudden goes out. It's not a case of where he had been sick or something."

Cantirino greets them and leads the immediate family into an empty conference room. Three sisters sit stiffly along one wall. The mother, a small, birdlike woman, sits opposite Cantirino, at the far end of a long walnut table. She sits sideways in her chair. No one looks directly at anyone else. The father sits to one side, overdressed in a heavy camel hair coat and a hat pulled down low. He periodically adjusts his brown-tinted glasses and stares at an empty blackboard.

Cantirino begins his pitch slowly, speaking gently. He says the doctors did all they could do. There is no hope. Repeating words already delivered to the family by a doctor, Cantirino says, "You son is dead. The brain is gone completely. He lost so much blood that there was no oxygen to the brain. And the brain, when it's deprived of oxygen, it dies."

Cantirino carefully punctuates his delivery with pauses, giving the family time to absorb the blows. He tells them an electroencephalogram, or EEG, a test of the brain's electrical activity, was done that day. He says it was "flat-line" for at least a half-hour—not even a spark of life.

There is a long silence. The father looks at the floor, glances at his fingernails. Then one of the sisters sobs. The two others immediately follow suit. The room fills with the sounds of their grief. The sisters shuffle out, hugging one another, leaving only the mother and father. The mother twists her wedding ring slowly. The room is silent.

"The only good that can come of this is that two people can have a new life," Cantirino says, now shifting to a positive tack. "It could be anybody from the age of three to fifty. It could be a woman with children; it could be a girl getting married."

The only sound is the humming of an electric clock. "I don't know if you know anybody on dialysis, but it's not very pleasant," he says. "This is the only chance these people have to have some sort of life." The victim's mother hardly moves. She stares at the metal legs on one of the plastic chairs. "It's a very hard thing to ask you people when you are losing a life, to give someone else a life," Cantirino says. "But it's the only time it can be done."

There is a long silence, finally broken by the father. "I know what it is all about, these things," he says. He speaks with a Spanish accent, slowly hefting each word like a heavy object. Cantirino, seeing he has gotten them over the first big hump, starts to lay out the situation in more detail. He says there will be an autopsy, as in any gunshot case. Giving up the kidneys will not affect any legal situation.

The father rises slowly, almost painfully. "I understand you perfectly," he says. His wife moves to his side. Cantirino hands the father a business card and tells them to go home, to think it over. The door closes behind the couple, leaving Cantirino alone in the silent room.

He retuns to the intensive care unit to tell the doctor that it will be at least two or three days before they get a decision. "They've just been told their son is dead," Cantirino says. "Regardless of what he did, he's dead. Now they have to accept this, to come to terms with it. Then they have to say okay—which I think they might, because we

didn't get a flat no. The father seems to be the strong one, yet the mother's the one who holds the key. You can see just by looking at her that no matter what he wants, she's the one who'll say, and whatever she says will go."

The family is due at noon, but they don't show up until midafternoon, and then it's just the three sisters. Cantirino repeats his litany, sitting with them in the same conference room. The three women are a still life. Each stares in a different direction—numb. Each has an elbow propped on the table and cups her chin in her palm. They seem sullen, even resentful. The shock seems to have dissipated somewhat, but it has been replaced by suspicion. They start to ask questions. Where will the kidneys go? Are they sold or given to anyone who needs them? When will the body be turned over to the family?

Cantirino carefully, patiently answers each question. The body will go to the Office of the Chief Medical Examiner of New York City. Because matching an organ donor with a recipient is first attempted locally, the kidneys will probably go to someone from Brooklyn. "It's people like us," he says.

A match is made from a list of potential recipients at New York's various transplant centers. The section is based on the length of time a patient has waited, the direness of the need, and the degree of tissue compatibility. "No one can buy a kidney, rich or poor," Cantirino says. "It's strictly through luck."

Thursday night the sisters return with their mother, who is now dressed in black. She sits in a chair in the hallway, beneath a cheap print of yellow flowers that hangs on the cinder block wall. The doctor stands to one side, talking quietly with a friend of the family's. Cantirino hands the consent form to the mother. She and her daughters read it slowly. At 7:50 P.M. the mother signs the paper, indicating that she speaks for her husband as well. The doctor signs the form and makes a final entry on the patient's chart: he pronounces him dead.

The family goes for a last look at the victim-turned-donor. There are a few sobs, but mostly silence. After several minutes they leave for the last time. The young man lies still. And endless line of heartbeats parades across a monitor over his head. The bellows hisses; his chest rises and falls. A radio somewhere squawks tinny rock and roll.

Cantirino does some paperwork and telephones the organ recovery team at the Health Science Center. Within a day the kidneys will be sutured into place in the abdomens of two people. Cantirino heads for the door, his job done. A nurse waves to him, smiling. "Happy hunting," she says.

Starting Time		Finishing Time	
Reading Time		Reading Rate	
Comprehension		Vocabulary	

Comprehension— Read the following questions and statements. For each one, put an *x* in the box before the option that contains the most complete or accurate answer. Check your answers in the Answer Key on page 108.

1. The best organ donors are frequently victims of
   - ☐ a. drug overdoses.
   - ☐ b. drownings and stabbings.
   - ☐ c. gunshot wounds and car accidents.
   - ☐ d. terminal illness.

2. Cantirino needs to get the permission of
   - ☐ a. all living relatives of the victim.
   - ☐ b. the victim's next of kin.
   - ☐ c. the victim's immediate family.
   - ☐ d. the victim's family and their lawyer.

3. Cantirino only approaches a victim's family after he is sure the victim is
   - ☐ a. under the age of fifty.
   - ☐ b. brain dead.
   - ☐ c. covered by medical insurance.
   - ☐ d. a legal resident of the state of New York.

4. Cantirino performs a task which is
   - ☐ a. tedious but necessary.
   - ☐ b. difficult but valuable.
   - ☐ c. financially draining.
   - ☐ d. ethically questionable.

5. Parents who donate the organs of their child take comfort in the knowledge that
   - ☐ a. their child is better off dead.
   - ☐ b. they will receive an autopsy report.
   - ☐ c. their actions will save the country money.
   - ☐ d. their actions will save the lives of other people.

6. Donating the organs of a brain-dead relative is a
   - ☐ a. gruesome act.
   - ☐ b. noble act.
   - ☐ c. selfish act.
   - ☐ d. mindless act.

7. Recipients of organ donations feel
   - ☐ a. confused by the process.
   - ☐ b. grateful for the chance at a new life.
   - ☐ c. guilty about benefitting from another's misfortune.
   - ☐ d. ostracized by society.

8. The mood which dominated the conference room was one of
   - ☐ a. hopelessness.
   - ☐ b. anguish.
   - ☐ c. regret.
   - ☐ d. fury.

9. Cantirino has great sympathy for
   - ☐ a. the doctors who treat accident victims.
   - ☐ b. people in need of organ donations.
   - ☐ c. victims of shootings.
   - ☐ d. people who refuse to donate organs.

10. Cantirino's statement that "the mother's the one who holds the key" is an example of
   - ☐ a. a simile.
   - ☐ b. a metaphor.
   - ☐ c. hyperbole.
   - ☐ d. literal language.

Comprehension Skills

1. recalling specific facts	6. making a judgment
2. retaining concepts	7. making an inference
3. organizing facts	8. recognizing tone
4. understanding the main idea	9. understanding characters
5. drawing a conclusion	10. appreciation of literary forms

Study Skills, Part One—Following is a passage with blanks where words have been omitted. Next to the passage are groups of five words, one group for each blank. Complete the passage by selecting the correct word for each of the blanks.

Mastering the Text, III

Another feature of the text you will want to explore is the index. Use it to obtain hard facts about the author and his presentation.

The Index. Every textbook contains a subject index. There may be other indexes too. An author's index, for example, may allow you to look up by ____(1)____ those

(1)   number   title
       name   page   chapter

authorities mentioned throughout the book. The index will also list their writings and works.

But the subject index is likely to be the only one included in your texts. It lists alphabetically aspects and ___(2)___ that were discussed in the text. The page number is given with each listing.

Based on classroom lectures or on some previous knowledge of yours in the field, ___(3)___ the author's treatment of one topic. Look through the index until you find a familiar entry. Go to the page listed and read the material. What kind of job has the author done? Did he discuss what you expected? Was his treatment too superficial? Make a couple more ___(4)___ if needed to see if the treatment is the same throughout the book. You may find that the text covers the field with more depth than you need; or the ___(5)___ may be the case—the text is too sketchy for you. You may need to find a book that gives a more comprehensive treatment.

Of course, you may be ___(6)___ to change texts and authors. The text you have may be the assigned book for the course. But you can use other texts. If needed, find one to supplement the one you deem to be lacking, one that you can read first to make the assigned text ___(7)___ to understand. Or you may wish to read a more extensive text, along with the assigned one, to broaden your knowledge. In other words, feed your interest in the subject—find a text that works for you and keeps your interest level high.

(2)   topics   countries
    names   places   circumstances

(3)   pursue   evaluate
    ignore   enjoy   follow

(4)   trips   challenges
    checks   friends   books

(5)   same   opposite
    ordinary   report   estimate

(6)   opposed   happy
    powerless   anxious   able

(7)   essential   harder
    faster   easier   optional

Study Skills, Part Two—Read the study skills passage again, paying special attention to the lesson being taught. Then, without looking back at the passage, complete each sentence below by writing in the missing word or words. Check the Answer Key on page 108 for the answers to Study Skills, Part One, and Study Skills, Part Two.

1. Every textbook contains a _____ index.

2. The index lists topics in _____ order.

3. Each listing is given with a page _____ .

4. Check to see how the author treats a subject with which you

   are _____ .

5. If the text does not suit your needs, you may wish to _____

   it with another.

16 | **Why Not Bicycle to Work?**

by Robert Petersen

Vocabulary—The five words below are from the story you are about to read. Study the words and their meanings. Then complete the ten sentences that follow, using one of the five words to fill in the blank in each sentence. Mark your answer by writing the letter of the word on the line before the sentence. Check your answers in the Answer Key on page 108.

A. disdained: regarded with contempt or scorn

B. prospective: likely to become or to occur

C. conspicuous: obvious; attracting attention

D. panoply: complete array

E. dissipating: driving away; dispersing

_____ 1. Some _____ cyclists worry excessively about the weather.

_____ 2. Cycling can be a good way of _____ tension.

_____ 3. Bright orange clothing makes a cyclist more _____ on the road.

_____ 4. Quiet back roads offer cyclists the best chance to view the _____ of seasons.

_____ 5. A _____ cyclist should consider what type of bicycle will best fit his or her needs.

_____ 6. Traditional parking lots, with their hefty fees, are _____ by people who cycle to work.

_____ 7. Cyclists wearing proper attire have little trouble _____ the heat generated by pedaling.

_____ 8. Bicycling enthusiasts offer a _____ of reasons why people should ride their bikes to work.

_____ 9. Some people fear they would feel _____ bicycling in a business suit.

_____ 10. Many employees at the National Institute of Health have _____ traditional commuting.

Cycle to work? "An appealing idea, but impractical" may be your first reaction. But is it? I and many of my coworkers at the National Institute of Health (N.I.H.) in Washington, D.C., do just that. What's more, many of us do it four out of five days of the week. Recently the Washington *Post* newspaper even proclaimed the bicycle the new status symbol at N.I.H.! The benefits? Better health, real savings in commuting costs, and the added bonus of cycling regularly year round.

The biggest bonus of all is the pleasure of cycling regularly and feeling better for doing so.

Let's examine how we do it and just how practical an idea it is. To begin with there's the question of distance. Just how far from work can you live and still use a bicycle as a means of commuting? I live five miles away and can make the trip comfortably in fifteen or twenty minutes. That includes several hefty hills and a few stoplights on the way. Up to ten miles away would still be well within the limits of reasonable commuting. And when you get there, there's no need to waste time trying to find a place to put the car or paying expensive parking fees. You can usually park in or near the building in which you work at no cost whatever.

What about the weather? In the Washington area summers are notoriously hot and humid. Winters, while they do not rival those of Maine or Minnesota, are still well below freezing part of the year. The solution? During the warmest part of the year, you are riding to work early in the day—before it's had a chance to warm up. I usually leave by about eight. By making maximum use of the wide range of gears of the modern lightweight bicycle it's possible to choose ratios that are minimally likely to overheat your personal radiator. I usually leave off my tie and suit jacket in warm weather, unbutton an extra button on my shirt, and can count on being suffiently "air-conditioned" to arrive at work without needing a shower. Since I can shower after returning home, I often make the return trip a more active one. I place my tie in my suitjacket pocket and carefully fold the jacket inside out—as you might for packing it in a suitcase. I then place the jacket on the luggage carrier secured by an elastic band or so-called shock cord (this can easily be obtained from your local cycle dealer). As a result my jacket and tie arrive as unruffled as I do.

During the winter I generally wear a coat over my business suit. A car coat is of convenient length for cycling and yet formal enough for attending a business lunch. My particular coat comes equipped with a hood attached to the collar which provides extra warmth and yet folds out of sight when not needed. On the very coldest days I add a wool sweater or suit vest for additional warmth. Part of the secret of being comfortable when cycling in winter is in wearing a hat and gloves. As the army discovered in World War II, the use of a hat and gloves greatly reduces heat losses and adds greatly to your comfort in cold weather. The other part of the secret lies in using your bicycle's gear ratios wisely. While in summer I choose among my gears for minimal effort so as to avoid becoming overheated, in winter I make my choice so as to insure enough effort to keep me warm. Hard as it may be to believe until you've actually tried it, the effort of cycling even in cold weather will keep you comfortably warm. And unlike the closed-in, overheated feeling you get in an automobile in winter, you're breathing really fresh air.

The only time I skip cycling to work is when it's actually raining or snowing when I start out in the morning. I suppose by a careful choice of rain gear I might even be able to ride in the rain. I generally avoid snow and icy road conditions because of the reduced stability of two-wheeled vehicles under these conditions. Despite eliminating riding when it's raining, snowing, or icy, I've been able to use my bicycle to commute more than 80 percent of the time. Even in more severe climates it's possible to cycle for much of the year.

People frequently ask me about traffic problems in commuting by bicycle. But remember, by cycling to work you're combining business with pleasure. What is the most efficient route by car is not necessarily the most efficient or most pleasant by bicycle. You're frequently better off choosing those secondary streets or roads disdained by the motorist as too narrow or slow for him. But by contrast, you're likely to find them fine for riding and delightfully free of carbon-monoxide fumes. You may even discover you're able to observe the world around you in a way you never could traveling by car. Even when it's necessary to use a major thoroughfare for part of the distance, I've found that there is frequently a shoulder out of the mainstream of traffic which is perfect for cycling. Motorists generally seem to give cyclists a wide berth. Perhaps it's because they associate bikes with children, but even on streets without shoulders, I've found that the typical motorist is usually considerate. He generally passes me with far more than enough room.

Why type of bicycle is best for commuting? I myself now use a fifteen-speed touring model equipped with dropped handlebars and a generator set. Before that I used a ten-speed bike with higher gear ratios, but I found it too highly geared for cycling with minimal effort in summer. My present bicycle is the same one I use for recreational riding. I chose the dropped handlebars because they offer a wider choice of riding positions than do other handlebar shapes. Most prospective cyclists have visions of themselves contorted into a pretzel-like shape if they use dropped bars. But as more experienced riders know, the advantage of that type of handlebar is that it provides a wider choice of riding positions for greater comfort and efficiency. You can ride with your hands on the upper or middle portion of the bars—in a more or less upright position—or with hands on the lower part of the bar for extra power.

While fifteen-gear ratios are convenient for touring under heavy load, ten-gear ratios with a sufficiently wide range of choices are more than adequate for commuting.

I personally use toe clips on the pedals, since this makes for more efficient pedaling. By keeping the straps loose enough, there is plenty of room for even heavy dress shoes to enable you to remove your feet quickly from the pedals as needed.

The generator set is especially convenient in winter when it is usually dark by late afternoon. I used to have a battery-operated headlamp, but the generator eliminates worries over dead batteries. I also have a rear light and a large red reflector on the back of the bicycle. To be absolutely certain of being seen, you can even add an orange visibility vest over your outer clothing. If that seems a bit too conspicuous, the reflector, reflecting tape on the bicycle, and the headlamp make it pretty difficult for any motorist to miss seeing you.

Because I often carry a briefcase to work, my bicycle has both front and rear luggage carriers, although one or the other would really be enough. Instead of a luggage carrier, a basket might be substituted with equal ease.

Another point sometimes brought up is any problems that might arise from riding in good clothing. Actually by wiping off excess oil from the chain drive and using fenders, this has never been a problem for me. Extra oil serves no useful purpose anyway, and lightweight fenders add very little to the weight of the bicycle.

Now that you're more than half convinced that cycling to work just might be practical after all, what are the health benefits? Dr. Kenneth Cooper, author of a best-selling book on physical fitness, *Aerobics*, highly recommends cycling as one of the best means of maintaining general fitness. By cycling as little as three miles to work and back at a pace just over fifteen miles per hour, it's possible to earn the thirty points a week Dr. Cooper suggests for optimal fitness. That level of fitness is, by the way, a higher level of physical well-being than Dr. Cooper found in nearly two-thirds of Air Force recruits—all men in their late teens or early twenties.

As for commuting costs, even if you figure as little as six cents per mile for operating the cheapest car, my ten miles of daily cycling save me at least 60 cents a day, $3 a week, or $150 a year. That's without taking into account extra auto-insurance costs, parking fees I don't pay, and other commuting expenses. In addition, using my bicycle for commuting has eliminated the need for a second car despite suburban living—a very substantial savings.

Last, but probably the biggest bonus of all, is the sheer pleasure of cycling regularly and feeling better for doing so. Perhaps I could discipline myself enough to exercise regularly, but bicycle commuting makes it a certainty. Cycling brings me closer to the world around me in a way that driving never would. I watch the changing seasons and the small events en route to my office in a way I never could while driving. Whether it's the arrival of the first birds from the south in spring or the changing colors as summer turns into fall, I am a more relaxed observer, better able to enjoy the panoply of seasons. And after the accumulated tensions of the workday, what better way to unwind than by pedaling home dissipating your tensions as you go?

Starting Time		Finishing Time	
Reading Time		Reading Rate	
Comprehension		Vocabulary	

Comprehension— Read the following questions and statements. For each one, put an *x* in the box before the option that contains the most complete or accurate answer. Check your answers in the Answer Key on page 108.

1. The limit of a reasonable commuting distance is about
   ☐ a. five miles.
   ☐ b. eight miles.
   ☐ c. ten miles.
   ☐ d. twelve miles.

2. Cycling to work offers
   ☐ a. a means of reducing highway accidents.
   ☐ b. physical and financial benefits.
   ☐ c. social and political advantages.
   ☐ d. a practical solution to the crime rate.

3. Before setting out for a morning commute by bicycle, a person should
   - ☐ a. consider the weather.
   - ☐ b. notify his or her employer.
   - ☐ c. consult his or her doctor.
   - ☐ d. calculate how much money will be needed to make the trip.

4. The purpose of the selection is to
   - ☐ a. promote the manufacture and sale of bicycles.
   - ☐ b. convince the public to exercise on a regular basis.
   - ☐ c. encourage more people to cycle to work.
   - ☐ d. advertise the need for bicycle trails.

5. Most people who bicycle to work
   - ☐ a. do so for monetary reasons.
   - ☐ b. enjoy their particular form of commuting.
   - ☐ c. are careless about basic safety rules.
   - ☐ d. endure teasing by their coworkers.

6. The author's claim that in the summer he arrives at work without needing a shower seems
   - ☐ a. reasonable.
   - ☐ b. impossible.
   - ☐ c. questionable.
   - ☐ d. miraculous.

7. A one-speed bicycle would
   - ☐ a. be sufficient to meet the needs of most commuters.
   - ☐ b. cost too much money to justify its use as a commuting vehicle.
   - ☐ c. not offer enough options for a comfortable commute.
   - ☐ d. reduce the risk of cycling accidents.

8. The author's personal knowledge and experience gives the selection a tone of
   - ☐ a. bravado.
   - ☐ b. boredom.
   - ☐ c. repetition.
   - ☐ d. authority.

9. The author is a
   - ☐ a. modest person.
   - ☐ b. persuasive person.
   - ☐ c. reclusive person.
   - ☐ d. forgiving person.

10. The author tries to appeal to the reader's
   - ☐ a. poetic impulses.
   - ☐ b. common sense.
   - ☐ c. desire for dignity.
   - ☐ d. compassion.

Comprehension Skills

1. recalling specific facts	6. making a judgment
2. retaining concepts	7. making an inference
3. organizing facts	8. recognizing tone
4. understanding the main idea	9. understanding characters
5. drawing a conclusion	10. appreciation of literary forms

Study Skills, Part One—Following is a passage with blanks where words have been omitted. Next to the passage are groups of five words, one group for each blank. Complete the passage by selecting the correct word for each of the blanks.

Mastering the Text, IV

You know from earlier discussions that previewing is the ___(1)___ reader's first step. Fortunately the organization of today's texts makes previewing quick and rewarding. Listed below are the steps to follow when previewing a textbook chapter.

PREREAD THE CHAPTER

1. Read the Title. As pointed out earlier, the title is the author's announcement of what is to come. It may in fact define the ___(2)___ of the entire chapter.

2. Read the Subheads. The subheads may list the author's three or four main points. They also may give a ___(3)___ to the significance of the forthcoming material. In either case, reading the subheads will give you a jump on the chapter.

(1)	slow	wise	
	advanced	adult	foolish

(2)	limits	forecast	
	outline	skill	ending

(3)	choice	clue	
	motive	statement	conclusion

3. Read the Illustrations. Don't just look at the illustrations, *read* them. The role of graphs, maps, and charts is to present in a ___(4)___ fashion data that might otherwise take hundreds of words to cover. Graphic aids often demonstrate a relationship between two facts. That relationship may be the very heart of the chapter—the base upon which the entire discussion is founded. Skipping over such obviously important aids in the name of saving time can decrease understanding. That in turn *increases* the time it takes to comprehend the material completely.

4. Read the Opening Paragraph. This helps you organize the material to come. Try to see what will be ___(5)___ of you when you read.

5. Read the Closing Paragraph. Capitalize on the author's ___(6)___ words, the statements that cap the chapter.

6. Skim through the Chapter. Get the feel of the presentation. Use typographical aids such as roman numerals, headlines, italics, and capital letters. Try to pick out the three or four ___(7)___ points to be covered. In that way, the sense of the lesson will be apparent to you even before you study it.

(4)		visual		vocal
	violent		written	audible

(5)		observed		received
	expected		thought	acquired

(6)		opening		favorite
	initial		hidden	parting

(7)		repeated		main
	simple		difficult	marginal

Study Skills, Part Two—Read the study skills passage again, paying special attention to the lesson being taught. Then, without looking back at the passage, complete each sentence below by writing in the missing word or words. Check the Answer Key on page 108 for the answers to Study Skills, Part One, and Study Skills, Part Two.

1. The _____ of today's texts makes previewing fast and helpful.

2. The title and _____ will give you an idea of what the chapter covers.

3. The belief that visual aids are not important for increasing understanding is

   _____ .

4. Read the opening and _____ paragraphs to give you a

   better understanding of the chapter's scope.

5. The last step in previewing is to _____ through the chapter.

17 | Bat Guano Can Make a Man Come Face-to-Face with His Values

by James Gorman

Vocabulary—The five words below are from the story you are about to read. Study the words and their meanings. Then complete the ten sentences that follow, using one of the five words to fill in the blank in each sentence. Mark your answer by writing the letter of the word on the line before the sentence. Check your answers in the Answer Key on page 108.

A. exemplary: worthy of imitation; commendable

B. lapse: slight failure

C. revulsion: strong and sudden disgust or loathing

D. carnage: massive slaughter

E. expiation: atonement; amends

_____ 1. Some people find that _____ for past sins is more difficult than they expected.

_____ 2. Bats have an _____ record when it comes to coexisting with humans.

_____ 3. The author admits to an occasional _____ of compassion when dealing with certain animals.

_____ 4. Many people feel an irrational _____ toward bats.

_____ 5. When it comes to cats, the author feels he has an _____ history.

_____ 6. Conservationists condemn the needless _____ caused by hunters.

_____ 7. The author's wife was apparently filled with _____ by the bat guano on her porch.

_____ 8. The author implies that his killing of a ruffed grouse represents a _____ of judgment on his part.

_____ 9. For the author, buying bat houses was an act of _____ for his previous deeds.

_____ 10. The author regrets the _____ for which he is responsible.

Being a conservationist used to be easy. You sent in your check to the Audubon Society and the Sierra Club. You hung out bird feeders. You hiked in the mountains and worked for the preservation of wild land, the nearer your summer house the better. You felt good, and nobody bothered you about bats. Bambi, Thumper, Dumbo—they

A smart person would take a bat over Peter Rabbit any day. A bat doesn't carry ticks and doesn't eat your lettuce.

were the animals that you were asked to support, not things that fly at night on leathery wings with that telltale heartbeat flutter.

Well, times have changed in the conservation game. When it comes to the currency of righteousness, money is getting tight. Now you're asked to save things you don't even like, or worse, to *like* things you don't even like. Like bats.

Bat Conservation International (BCI), which is devoted to just what its name says, has gathered 1,200 members since it was founded in 1982. And in the past year it has sold more than 3,000 bat houses. Yes, bat houses. These are wooden constructions in which bats can snuggle up during the day and hang from their feet, snoozing away like the little cutie-pies BCI says most of them really are, until they crawl out at dusk, fly by your ear, and scare the conservation right out of you. If you harbor irrational fear of bats, that is. You shouldn't. Most of the myths you've heard about bats are false. Vampires do not turn into bats. A bat won't get tangled in a woman's hair (unless she's got a lot of bugs in there and the bat is really hungry). And although devils are often portrayed with bats' wings, bats are not devils in any theological sense. (Angels are commonly drawn with feathered birds' wings, which I suppose makes Lucifer's transit from heaven to hell less of a fall and more of a taxonomic leap, from Aves to Mammalia.)

Bats rarely have rabies. I know it would be nicer to say they never have rabies, but the truth is the truth. Fewer than one bat in 200 has rabies, according to zoologist Merlin Tuttle, the founder of BCI, and the bats that are sick are almost never aggressive. In the 40 years for which records have been kept in the United States, only ten people are thought to have caught rabies from bats, a small fraction of the people killed *every* year by martinis. The trouble is that most people like martinis a lot more than they do bats—which just proves that people have no taste. They also like bunny rabbits, which carry tularemia and ticks and eat up all your lettuces. (The more I garden, the more I sympathize with Mr. McGregor and his wife; I too would have put Peter's father in a pie.) Bats, on the other hand, if you have them in your yard, will be eating not your lettuces but your mosquitoes—a main selling point of BCI's bat houses.

The true character of the bat, according to BCI, is that

of an exemplary ecological citizen, and a ubiquitous one. Bats make up nearly one quarter of mammalian species. They eat enormous numbers of insects. In fact, the 20 or so million bats that live in the world's biggest bat cave, in Texas, eat a quarter-million pounds of insects a night. The big fruit-eating bats are necessary for the survival of many tropical plants, if not of the tropical forests themselves. A bat is the symbol of Bacardi rum. However, it is José Cuervo who should really be probat, since nectar-feeding bats (they're like hummingbirds; well, sort of like hummingbirds) are the main pollinators of the agave plant, from which tequila comes.

It's BCI's job to get all this information out, to stop misguided attacks on bats, save bat caves from destruction and vandalism, and sell a few bat houses, which, in a small way, provide some new habitat for bats. And BCI does a good job, except for one lapse. Its brochures don't quote Randall Jarrell. He wrote a wonderful children's book called *The Bat-Poet*, which begins, "Once upon a time there was a bat—a little light brown bat, the color of coffee with cream in it." This bat becomes a poet and in his verse immortalizes chipmunks, owls, mockingbirds, and finally, bats. Reciting his poem on a newborn bat and his mother (bats, even in children's books, have an oral, not a written, tradition), he says,

> "All night, in happiness, she hunts and flies.
> Her high sharp cries
> Like shining needlepoints of sound . . . "

And later,

> "Her baby drinks the milk she makes him
> In moonlight or starlight, in mid-air."

Nothing in BCI's literature could possibly do as much for bats as one reading of Jarrell's book, which also does its bit for poets. Writes Jarrell, "The trouble isn't making poems; the trouble's finding somebody that will listen to them."

If all that Tuttle and Jarrell and BCI say is true, then bats are wonderful indeed. And if that's so—and this is the question that worries me—what does that make somebody who shoots bats, or, not to be too hard upon myself, someone who used to shoot bats?

I don't think of myself as a horrible person. I think of myself as a good person, an environmenally moral person. Sometimes I even see myself as leaning toward noble, like Lancelot in the days when he was still able to keep his hands off Guinevere. I think most people who know me would agree that I'm conversation-minded. My whole family is. We tell our daughters to put periwinkles back when they're done carrying them around in their pails. Often we carry snakes to somebody else's yard when we don't want them in our yard. (It's animals I said I was nice to, not my neighbors.) Nonetheless, I have killed bats. Trying to hold on to these two conflicting views of myself (conservationist/bat killer), I've ended up suffering from what's known in the bat business as cognitive dissonance. I realize that an outsider might think the point here should be the bats' suffering and not mine. But did Lady Macbeth worry about Duncan or about getting her hands clean? Why should I be any better than a Shakespearean character? What I want to know is, to put it bluntly, am I a good guy or a bad guy? And if a guy as good as me is bad, is anybody good these days?

But I'm getting ahead of myself. Let me describe the crime: The bats I went after were under a porch roof on a log cabin in upstate New York that my family and I share with them in the summer. They were leaving a lot of bat guano on the porch floor. Consequently, my wife wanted them dead. I know of few stronger supporters of conservation than my wife. However, she does feel that conservation has its limits. I think her view is that conservation is the opposite of charity: home (our home, anyway) is not where it begins, but where it ends.

To defend our home, which is what my daddy taught me was a man's job, I sat outside with a single-shot .22 caliber rifle and a box of cartridges filled with dust shot. This was at dusk, when the bats started to peek out from the rafters. I had a flashlight, and whenever I saw a bat, I fired away. I didn't do too well at hitting the bats—I think I killed two or three over the course of several twilights—but I did a nice job of shooting up the roof. Finally I gave up, overcome with revulsion for not taking them on the wing. We all gave up. For the past year or two we've spent the mornings of our vacations sweeping bat guano off the porch so that our kids don't crawl in it.

I'm not a vicious person. (I've never killed a cat. Then you really get letters.) But having thought about it, and since this whole bat business has come up I have thought about it, I realize that there are a lot of things that, to keep *my* life going the way I like it, I kill. Like mosquitoes. Of course, we all kill mosquitoes, but mosquitoes are invertebrates, and we usually don't worry a whole lot about the lower animals. The problems come when I start looking at what kind of carnage I've caused in my own phylum. I kill fish, but I always eat them, as I did the ruffed grouse (once, I killed a ruffed grouse only once). I killed a snake

when I was a boy, but it had bitten me. I didn't eat the snake, but I did eat a few of the frogs I killed—their legs, anyway. But I haven't killed frogs in years.

Other than those, and leaving out invertebrates, there were the laboratory rats in high school and the flying squirrels. Actually, *I* didn't kill the squirrels; I had them killed. They lived inside the cabin with the bat-inflicted porch. We got the farmer up the road to come sit in our living room and shoot them one by one with the same dust shot I used on the bats.

I think that's it, the carnage I mean, not counting mice—I can't believe we have to count mice. I tried to kill a porcupine once because it was gnawing on the cabin, but it got away. I think if you know how fast porcupines move, you know that a man from whom they can get away is no threat to Sylvester Stallone. But there's a lot of bad-guy room before you get to Rambo (or is he supposed to be a good guy?) and I just don't know where I fit in. Sometimes I think I'm just an average homeowner. Other times I feel like Raskolnikov.

So I joined BCI and bought two bat houses. For expiation. Also, I've resolved not to shoot any more bats. I want to feel clean again. What I will do, however, is put up wire screening in the fall to exclude them from our cabin's rafters. This won't be so bad: they'll have the bat houses to live in. I'm also going to leave the frogs and snakes alone, but I can't make any promises about the mice and the squirrels. It's possible that certain small mammals and I will be forever at odds. You see, I think my wife's analysis of conservation is correct. I think, ethically, the deal we should strike with the rest of creation is that we'll work to keep some land around for them, whatever kind of habitat they like, wetlands, caves, lawns—I'm willing to give them lawns—but not houses (I mean real houses, *people* houses). We get to keep those—porches included.

Starting Time		*Finishing Time*	
Reading Time		*Reading Rate*	
Comprehension		*Vocabulary*	

Comprehension— Read the following questions and statements. For each one, put an *x* in the box before the option that contains the most complete or accurate answer. Check your answers in the Answer Key on page 108.

1. Bats rarely
   □ a. sleep during the day.
   □ b. hang from their feet.
   □ c. have rabies.
   □ d. use bat houses.

2. Bats are useful to have around because they
   □ a. fertilize plants.
   □ b. produce tularemia.
   □ c. eat insects.
   □ d. frighten off snakes.

17: BAT GUANO CAN MAKE A MAN COME FACE-TO-FACE WITH HIS VALUES

3. As a child, the author
□ a. knew little about bats.
□ b. loved bats.
□ c. joined the BCI.
□ d. built a bat house.

4. Environmental conservation is
□ a. no longer as important as it once was.
□ b. an idea without merit.
□ c. losing popularity among homeowners.
□ d. not an easy principle to live by.

5. The author's wife dislikes
□ a. chipmunks.
□ b. bat guano.
□ c. rabbits.
□ d. dragonflies.

6. With regard to animal protection, the author's record is
□ a. commendable.
□ b. better than average.
□ c. ghastly.
□ d. unusual.

7. Members of BCI
□ a. tend to be Europeans.
□ b. are fans of Randall Jarrell.
□ c. try to correct common misconceptions about bats.
□ d. also fight to protect snakes, frogs, and fish.

8. The tone of the last paragraph is
□ a. conciliatory.
□ b. confrontational.
□ c. pessimistic.
□ d. embarrassed.

9. The author has
□ a. an active fantasy life.
□ b. a guilty conscience.
□ c. an aggressive personality.
□ d. a sadistic streak.

10. This selection contains several
□ a. literary allusions.
□ b. rhymes.
□ c. change-of-names.
□ d. fictional statements.

Comprehension Skills

1. recalling specific facts
2. retaining concepts
3. organizing facts
4. understanding the main idea
5. drawing a conclusion
6. making a judgment
7. making an inference
8. recognizing tone
9. understanding characters
10. appreciation of literary forms

Study Skills, Part One—Following is a passage with blanks where words have been omitted. Next to the passage are groups of five words, one group for each blank. Complete the passage by selecting the correct word for each of the blanks.

Marking the Text

If you ___(1)___ your textbook you will want to write in it. Marking the text as you read is creative reading—it is motivating and stimulating. It can be the most creative reading you do.

Don't make the mistake of some students—that of frequent highlighting. Many students feel that they should highlight important facts and information. But as they read, almost everything they encounter seems to be important and ___(2)___ of being highlighted. If you look at a book owned by a student who has this habit, you will find that almost a third of every chapter is marked. In such a case, the highlighting is so distracting that the eye actually seeks out the ___(3)___ passages to read.

In other words, you must mark selectively. Highlight only those passages that are of extreme importance, and use some more methods of marking the text that are effective and not distracting. For instance, if you wish

(1)	rent		own	
	lease	borrow		steal

(2)	worthy		wary	
	hopeful	desirous		afraid

(3)	bright		dull	
	unmarked	marked		scribbled

to set off an important line or passage, use the abbreviation *imp.* in the margin. You can also use circles, numbers, and brackets to effectively ___(4)___ your text.

Brackets are used in much the same way as highlighting to mark off very ___(5)___ statements. Look for such statements at the start of each new division. A strong summary statement is a good candidate for bracketing too. But remember, use brackets sparingly.

Circles and numbers are used to indicate important series and enumerations. Circle the key word that begins the series, then number the items in the series. You do that to help you find the list later. Many times explanations and details accompany a list, and the items may be sentences, paragraphs, or even ___(6)___ apart.

Abbreviations are used to indicate the principal statement *(imp.)* of the whole lesson; a major illustration *(ill.)* that helps the reader ___(7)___ an essential concept; and a conclusion *(con.)* based on facts and data included in the chapter.

(4) mark recall destroy improve write

(5) frequent important scarce biased true

(6) pages chapters books inches rooms

(7) regret predict understand enjoy control

Study Skills, Part Two—Read the study skills passage again, paying special attention to the lesson being taught. Then, without looking back at the passage, complete each sentence below by writing in the missing word or words. Check the Answer Key on page 108 for the answers to Study Skills, Part One, and Study Skills, Part Two.

1. Marking the text as you read can be the most _____ reading you do.

2. Don't make the mistake of highlighting too _____ .

3. _____ may be used to mark off statements at the beginning and end of each division.

4. Circle the key words, and _____ the items in a series.

5. Imp., ill., and con. are _____ you may use.

18 | Children of the A-Bomb

by Arata Osada

Vocabulary—The five words below are from the story you are about to read. Study the words and their meanings. Then complete the ten sentences that follow, using one of the five words to fill in the blank in each sentence. Mark your answer by writing the letter of the word on the line before the sentence. Check your answers in the Answer Key on page 108.

A. abruptly: suddenly

B. obsessed: intensely preoccupied

C. pitiable: arousing or deserving compassion

D. pessimistic: gloomy

E. stimulates: encourages; rouses to action

_____ 1. For days, victims of the atomic bomb were in _____ condition.

_____ 2. The bomb exploded _____, killing hundreds of thousands of people.

_____ 3. Many victims were _____ with the thought of getting a drink of water.

_____ 4. Someone who has lived through an atomic bombing has cause to be _____ about the future of mankind.

_____ 5. The narrator made a _____ attempt to eat a white rice ball.

_____ 6. The fleeing townspeople were _____ with the notion of getting away from the blast area.

_____ 7. The courage of one person sometimes _____ others to be brave.

_____ 8. People with a _____ view of the world expect another atomic bomb to be dropped.

_____ 9. The need for energy _____ scientists to experiment with atoms.

_____ 10. The narrator's homeward journey stopped _____ at the point where the iron bridge had collapsed.

Can it really be said that a thing which takes several hundred thousand human lives at one time is true scientific development?

Ah, that instant! I felt as though I had been struck on the back with something like a big hammer, and thrown into boiling oil. For some time I was unconscious. When I abruptly came to again, everything around me was smothered in black smoke; it was all like a dream or something that didn't make sense. My chest hurt, I could barely breathe, and I thought "This is the end!" I pressed my chest tightly and lay face down on the ground, and ever so many times I called for help: "Mother!" "Mother!" "Father!" but of course in that place there was no answer from Mother, no answer from Father.

I recovered my senses. Through a darkness like the bottom of hell I could hear the voices of the other students calling for their mothers. I could barely sense the fact that the students seemed to be running away from that place. I immediately got up, and without any definite idea of escaping I just frantically ran in the direction they were all taking. By this time everything had long since changed to white smoke. The place where I had been working was Tanaka-cho, a little more than 600 yards from the center of the explosion. Although I should have been at a place straight in from Tsurumi Bridge, I seemed to have been blown a good way to the north, and I felt as though the directions were all changed around.

At the base of the bridge, inside a big cistern that had been dug out there, was a mother weeping and holding above her head a naked baby that was burned bright red all over its body, and another mother was crying and sobbing as she gave her burned breast to her baby. In the cistern the students stood with only their heads above the water and their two hands, which they clasped as they imploringly cried and screamed, calling their parents. But every single person who passed was wounded, all of them, and there was no one to turn to for help. The singed hair on people's heads was frizzled up and whitish, and covered with dust—from their appearance you couldn't believe that they were human creatures of this world.

Looking at these people made me think suddenly "It can't be possible that I—." I looked at my two hands and found them covered with blood, and from my arms something that looked like rags was hanging and inside I could see the healthy-looking flesh with its mingled colors of white, red, and black.

I could feel my face gradually swelling up, but there was nothing I could do about it, and when some of my friends suggested that we try to return to our homes in the suburbs, I set out with them. As we walked along, fires were blazing high on both sides of us, and my back was painfully hot. From inside the wreckage of the houses we would hear screaming voices calling "Help!" and then the flames would swallow up everything. A child of about six, all covered with blood, holding a kitchen pot in his arms, was facing a burning house, stamping his feet and screaming something. I was in such a state that I didn't even know what to do about myself, so I could hardly attempt to be much help to him, and there was nothing to do but let him go.

I wonder what happened to those people? Those people trapped under the houses? The four of us, simply obsessed with the idea of reaching home at the earliest possible minute, hurried along in just the opposite direction from that of the fleeing townspeople—straight toward the center of the blast area. However when we came to Inarimachi, we found that the iron bridge had collapsed and we could not go any farther. We turned about there and ran toward Futaba Hill. When we were close to the foot of the hill I simply couldn't make my legs carry me another step.

"Wait for me. Please wait for me," I said, and practically crawling, I finally reached the foot of the hill. Luckily there were some kind soldiers from a medical unit there, and they carried me up the hill to a place where I could lie down. There they gave me first aid treatment right away. It seemed that I had received a terrific blow on the back of my head, and there were fragments of roof tile left there. They pulled these out and bandaged the wound for me.

"You must lie there quietly. Your teacher will surely be along any minute now to take care of you," they said to comfort me.

But no matter how long I waited, my teacher didn't come. (Our teachers themselves were severely wounded; some of them died on the afternoon of the sixth, and all of them were dead by the next day.)

Finally the soldiers couldn't wait any longer, and they carried us one by one on their backs down to the barracks at the foot of the hill. A Red Cross flag was waving there. They carried us inside and asked the doctors to take care of us right away. But there were so many wounded people that we had to wait a very long time for our turn to come. In the meantime my strength was exhausted and I couldn't even keep myself standing up. At last they gave us treatment, and we spent the night there. The big buildings in the city were burning steadily, bright red against the dark sky. As the night wore on, the barracks gradually filled to overflowing with moaning voices—over in one corner someone shrieking "Bring me a straw mat if there's nothing better," and here a patient rolling about even on top of people too badly burned to move.

The first night came to an end. From earliest morning

voices calling "water, water," came from every side. I too was so thirsty I could hardly bear it. Inside the barracks there was a sink with water in it. Even though I knew that all sorts of things drained into it and the water was dirty, I scooped up some of that milk-coffee-colored water with my shoe and drank it. Maybe it is because I was normally healthy—anyway my mind was perfectly clear even though I had that severe wound, and since I knew there was a stream running right behind the barracks, I got up and took that shoe and went and drank and drank. And after that any number of times I brought water and gave it to the people who were lying near me and to the soldiers who were wounded.

My friends, and the other people too, could not move after they once lay down. Their backs and arms and legs were all slippery where the skin had peeled off, and even if I wanted to raise them up, there was no place I could take hold of them. From about noon of the second day people began to come in a few at a time. I got a white rice ball from those people, but since my face was burned and I couldn't open my mouth very well, I spilled the grains of rice all around when I tried to eat, and only a little bit of it finally ended up in my mouth. By the third day I too was all swollen up, even around my eyes, and I had to lie there beside my friends unable to move at all.

My father and four or five of our neighbors were searching around for me day after day and finally on the evening of the third day they discovered me in one corner of the barracks at the foot of Futaba Hill. On my blouse there was sewn a name tag that my father had written for me; the letters had been burned out just as though that part of the cloth had been eaten away by moths, and it was by this that they were able to find me.

"Atchan. This is Father."

When he said that, I was so happy that I couldn't say a word—I could only nod my head. My swollen eyes wouldn't open, so I couldn't see my father's face. This is how I was rescued.

Even now the scars of those wounds remain over my whole body. On my head, my face, my arms, my legs, and my chest. As I stroke these black-reddish raised scars on my arms, and every time I look in a mirror at this face of mine which is not like my face, and think that never again will I be able to see my former face and that I have to live my life forever in this condition, it becomes too sad to bear.

At the time I lost hope for the future. And not for a single moment could I get rid of the feeling that I had become a cripple. And naturally, for that reason I hated to meet people. And along with that, I couldn't get out

of my mind the thought that so many of my good friends, and the teachers who had taken care of me so lovingly, had died under such pitiable circumstances, and I was continually choked with tears. No matter what I thought about, I was likely to be suspicious, and I took a pessimistic attitude toward everything. And my voice, which until now had been a pleasant one that all my friends liked, was lost all at once and became a hoarse voice without any volume. Every time I think about these things, my chest feels as though a terribly tight band is closing around it.

But with human beings, it isn't only a beautiful outward appearance that is good. True beauty, worthy of a human being, takes away an ugly appearance and makes it into a splendid one. When I first realized that, my spirit softened somewhat. At the present time, with a fresh hope for life, and studying earnestly to discipline both my body and spirit, I cannot help seeking the inner sort of beauty which comes from a cultivated mind.

Science—what in the world is this science? Can it really be said that a thing which takes several hundred thousand human lives at one time is true scientific development? No, science ought to be something that to the very last stimulates those advancements of civilization which are beneficial to mankind. Moreover, the mission of science is to raise the standard of living of mankind. It ought never to be such a thing as would annihilate the life of mankind. It is also obvious that the power of the atom, instead of being thus used as a means of making human beings lose their lives, ought to be turned to the advancement of human civilization. It is my hope that in the future such a tragic event as this will never make a second appearance in this world. And I want things to work out so that atomic energy will be the power which will give birth to a peaceful world. I believe there is no necessity for mankind to experience directly such suffering.

The atomic bomb dropped on the city of Hiroshima, Japan, on August 6, 1945, destroyed 4.7 square miles of the city. More than 92,000 persons were dead or missing. Others died later from the effects of atomic radiation.

Starting Time		Finishing Time	
Reading Time		Reading Rate	
Comprehension		Vocabulary	

Comprehension— Read the following questions and statements. For each one, put an x in the box before the option that contains the most complete or accurate answer. Check your answers in the Answer Key on page 108.

1. The narrator had sustained a terrible blow to the
   - ☐ a. back.
   - ☐ b. neck.
   - ☐ c. head.
   - ☐ d. chest.

2. The narrator realized that she was badly injured after she
   - ☐ a. could not keep up with her friends.
   - ☐ b. compared herself to the other victims.
   - ☐ c. could not satisfy her thirst.
   - ☐ d. tried to help the trapped victims.

3. After the blast, the narrator first tried to get to
   - ☐ a. Futaba Hill.
   - ☐ b. Tanaka-cho.
   - ☐ c. her parents' home.
   - ☐ d. her school.

4. Which of the following statements best expresses the main idea of the selection?
   - ☐ a. The power of the atom is a regrettable scientific discovery.
   - ☐ b. Mankind can never expect to benefit from the use of atomic power.
   - ☐ c. The misuse of science cannot be justified.
   - ☐ d. Intellectual accomplishments are superior to physical accomplishments.

5. An atomic blast causes not only destruction, suffering, and death, but also
   - ☐ a. makes rescue almost impossible.
   - ☐ b. causes people to become selfish.
   - ☐ c. transforms victims into volunteers.
   - ☐ d. reduces everything to rubble.

6. Those who could walk were unable to help the trapped victims. This must have been
   - ☐ a. held against them.
   - ☐ b. cruel and selfish.
   - ☐ c. difficult to bear.
   - ☐ d. merciful and humane.

7. The victims of atomic radiation all seem to
   - ☐ a. require sleep.
   - ☐ b. walk slowly.
   - ☐ c. crave water.
   - ☐ d. fear noise.

8. The atmosphere at the beginning of the selection is one of
   - ☐ a. disgust and revulsion.
   - ☐ b. shock and helplessness.
   - ☐ c. shame and sorrow.
   - ☐ d. suffering and indifference.

9. At the barracks, the narrator wanted to
   - ☐ a. help fellow victims.
   - ☐ b. die.
   - ☐ c. seek revenge.
   - ☐ d. remain anonymous.

10. The greater part of the selection is written in the form of a
    - ☐ a. political essay.
    - ☐ b. fictional account.
    - ☐ c. government report.
    - ☐ d. descriptive narrative.

Comprehension Skills

1. recalling specific facts	6. making a judgment
2. retaining concepts	7. making an inference
3. organizing facts	8. recognizing tone
4. understanding the main idea	9. understanding characters
5. drawing a conclusion	10. appreciation of literary forms

Study Skills, Part One—Following is a passage with blanks where words have been omitted. Next to the passage are groups of five words, one group for each blank. Complete the passage by selecting the correct word for each of the blanks.

Comprehension and Reading, I

Reading is both a visual and a mental skill. The visual parts involve seeing the words and _____ the eyes. The mental activities call for recognizing the organization of the letters and understanding the _____ . The first skills needed for thorough comprehension are word recognition skills.

(1)
checking   washing
rolling   closing   moving

(2)
person   thought
word   mind   reason

Once the word has been seen, it must be recognized if it is to be understood. We recognize words by remembering them, pronouncing them, or analyzing them. The words we recall are those in our sight vocabulary. Those are the words we see often enough to recognize on sight. You may recall ___(3)___ lists of "sight words" in the early grades of school. Good readers—sight readers—have developed a large vocabulary of words that they recognize at once when reading. Such readers slow down to sound out or pronounce only when they come to a new and ___(4)___ word. Frequently in reading clinics and reading improvement courses, projectors are used to flash sight words on the screen for fractions of a second. That training is designed to enhance and reinforce the reader's stock of sight words.

The second way we recognize words is by pronouncing them. We do this for words that are not part of our sight vocabulary but are in our ___(5)___ vocabulary. They are words we recognize when we hear them spoken aloud. Our knowledge of phonics helps us to pronounce unfamiliar words—that is why phonics skills are valuable.

The third technique we use in word recognition is analysis, which means breaking a word down into recognizable ___(6)___ . Our knowledge of syllabication and word parts helps us do this.

Reading programs that feature only one ___(7)___ of attacking new words shortchange the student. To become competent readers, we need to use all the recognition skills.

(3)   dividing   memorizing
        reading   spelling   producing

(4)   dramatic   abstract
        exciting   interesting   unfamiliar

(5)   listening   reading
        spelling   working   writing

(6)   partners   parts
        looks   lessons   places

(7)   outline   picture
        question   situation   method

Study Skills, Part Two—Read the study skills passage again, paying special attention to the lesson being taught. Then, without looking back at the passage, complete each sentence below by writing in the missing word or words. Check the Answer Key on page 108 for the answers to Study Skills, Part One, and Study Skills, Part Two.

1. Reading is both a visual and a _____ skill.

2. The words we remember are those in our _____ vocabulary.

3. Good readers have a large vocabulary of words that they

   _____ immediately when reading.

4. Our knowledge of _____ helps us to pronounce unfamiliar words.

5. The technique called _____ means breaking a word into

   recognizable parts.

Alive, I

by Piers Paul Read

Vocabulary—The five words below are from the story you are about to read. Study the words and their meanings. Then complete the ten sentences that follow, using one of the five words to fill in the blank in each sentence. Mark your answer by writing the letter of the word on the line before the sentence. Check your answers in the Answer Key on page 108.

A. extricate: to free from an entanglement

B. desolation: loneliness and misery

C. superficial: on or near the surface; not deep

D. contemplated: considered; pondered

E. obliterating: destroying or wiping out

_____ 1. Some of the survivors were able to _____ themselves from the wreckage.

_____ 2. After Bobby Francois climbed out of the plane, he _____ his situation.

_____ 3. The night soon came, _____ all views of the mountains.

_____ 4. The boys with _____ wounds helped those who were more seriously hurt.

_____ 5. Moncho Sabella could not _____ Lagurara from the cockpit.

_____ 6. The boys _____ Carlos Valetas' fate as he disappeared into the valley.

_____ 7. As Carlitos Páez and Bobby Francois surveyed the scene, a feeling of _____ flooded over them.

_____ 8. Lagurara found his desire for water _____ all other thoughts.

_____ 9. From outside the plane, the crash site seemed one of pure _____ .

_____ 10. The cut on Susana Parrado's forehead was not just a _____ one.

As the plane had hurtled down the valley, Canessa had braced himself for the impact, thinking that in a moment he would die. He did not pray but calculated in his mind the speed of the plane and the force with which it would hit the rock. Then suddenly he was conscious that the plane was no longer moving.

He shouted, "It's stopped!"

Their plane crashed high in the Andes Mountains. For the survivors, an incredible ordeal had just begun.

and then turned to the boy who sat beside him and asked him if he were all right. The boy was in a state of shock. He nodded and Canessa left him to help his friend Daniel Maspons extricate himself from his seat. Then the two of them started to help others. At first they thought that they were the only two who were not injured, for all around them they could hear cries for help, but others began to emerge from the wreckage. First came Gustavo Zerbino, then the team captain, Marcelo Pérez. Pérez had a bruised face and a pain in his side, but as captain of the team he immediately took it upon himself to organize the rescue of those trapped in the wreckage, while two medical students, Canessa and Zerbino, did what they could for the injured.

Immediately after the plane had stopped, some of the younger boys, smelling the gasoline fumes and fearing that the plane might explode or catch fire, had jumped out the gaping hole at the back. They found themselves up to their thighs in snow. Bobby Francois, the first to leave the plane, climbed onto a suitcase and lit a cigarette. "We've had it," he said to Carlitos Páez, who had followed him out into the snow.

The scene was one of the utmost desolation. All around them was snow and beyond, on three sides, the sheer gray walls of the mountains. The plane had come to a halt on a slight tilt, facing down the valley where the mountains were much farther away and now partly obscured by gray clouds. It was bitterly cold, and many of the boys were in their shirt sleeves. Some wore sports coats and others blazers. No one was dressed for subzero temperatures, and few suitcases could be seen which might provide extra clothes.

As they looked back up the mountain for their lost luggage, this group of younger boys saw a figure staggering down the mountainside. As it drew nearer, they recognized one of their friends, Carlos Valeta, and shouted to him, calling him to come in their direction. Valeta seemed unable to see or hear them. At each step he sank up to his thighs in the snow, and only the steepness of the hill enabled him to make any progress at all. The boys could see that his course would not lead him to the plane, so they shouted yet more frantically to attract his attention. Two, Páez and Storm, even tried to go out to meet him, but it was impossible to walk in the snow,

particularly uphill. They were trapped and could only watch helplessly as Valeta stumbled down into the valley. For a moment it seemed as if he might have heard them and was changing direction toward the plane, but then he slipped. His wide stride became a tumble, and his body slithered helplessly down the side of the mountain until he finally disappeared in the snow.

Inside the plane, the handful of boys who were able tried to pry away the seats which trapped so many of the wounded. In the thin air of the mountains it took double the energy and effort, and those who had suffered only superficial injuries were still in a state of shock.

Canessa knelt down to examine the crushed body of a woman which at first he could not recognize. It was Eugenia Parrado, and she was dead. Beside her lay Susana Parrado, who was semiconscious and alive but seriously injured. Blood poured out of a gash in her forehead and blinded one eye. Canessa wiped away the blood, so that she could see, and then laid her down on the small part of the floor that was not cluttered with seats.

Near her was Abal. He too was severely injured, with an open wound in his scalp. He was semiconscious and, as Canessa knelt to treat him as best he could, Abal took hold of his hand, saying, "Please don't leave me, old man, please don't leave me." There were so many others crying for help that Canessa could not stay with him. He called to Zerbino to tend to Abal and moved on to Parrado, who had been thrown out of his seat and lay senseless at the front of the plane. His face was covered with bruises and blood and Canessa thought that he was dead. He knelt and felt for a pulse; a faint beating of the heart registered on his fingertips. Parrado was still alive, but it seemed impossible that he could live for long, and since nothing could be done to help him, he was given up for dead.

Besides Eugenia Parrado, only two other passengers in the fuselage had died instantly. These were the Nicolas; both had been flung forward into the luggage compartment side by side and had died at once.

For the time being their bodies were left where they were, and the two medical students returned to do what they could for the living. They made bandages of the antimacassars from the backs of the seats, but for many of the injuries these were quite inadequate. One boy, Rafael Echavarren, had had the calf of his right leg torn off and twisted around to cover the shin. The bone was entirely exposed. Zerbino took hold of the bleeding muscle, pulled it around to its proper place, and then bound up his leg with a white shirt.

Another boy—Enrique Platero—came up to Zerbino with a steel tube sticking into his stomach. Zerbino was appalled, but he remembered from his lessons in medical psychology that a good doctor always instills confidence into his patient, so he looked Platero straight in his eye and, with as much conviction as he could put into his tone of voice, said, "Well, Enrique, you look all right."

"Do you think so?" said Platero, pointing to the piece of steel in his stomach. "And what about this?"

"Don't worry about that," said Zerbino. "You're perfectly strong, so come and give me a hand with these seats."

Platero seemed to accept this. He turned toward the seats and, as he did so, Zerbino grabbed hold of the tube, put his knee against Platero's body, and pulled. The piece of steel came out, and with it came almost six inches of what Zerbino took to be Platero's intestine.

Platero, his attention once more upon his stomach, contemplated his projecting innards with some dismay, but before he had time to complain, Zerbino said to him, "Now look here, Enrique, you may think you're in a bad way, but there are plenty of others much worse off than you are, so don't be a coward, and just come and help. Tie that up with a shirt, and I'll see to it later."

Without complaint Platero did as Zerbino had told him.

The plane had crashed at about half past three in the afternoon. Because of the clouds the light was already somber, and around four o'clock it began to snow. The few flakes which fell at first grew into a flurry and then fell thickly, obliterating the view of the mountains. In spite of the snow, Marcelo Pérez directed that the wounded should be carried out so that those who were fit could clear the tangled seats from the floor of the Fairchild. This was intended as a temporary measure; they all felt sure that by now the plane would have been reported missing and help would be on the way.

They realized that the rescue might be made easier if they could transmit signals from the radio. The entrance to the pilots' cabin was blocked by the wall of seats which had piled up at the top of the passenger compartment, but sounds of life could be heard from the other side, so one of the calmer boys, Moncho Sabella, decided to try to reach the pilots from the outside.

It was almost impossible to walk on the snow, but he discovered that he could use seat cushions as stepping-stones to the front of the plane. The nose had been crushed by the descent, but it was not difficult to climb up and look into the cockpit through the door to the front luggage compartment.

There he discovered that Ferradas and Lagurara were trapped in their seats, with the instruments of the airplane embedded in their chests. Ferradas was dead, but Lagurara was alive and conscious and, seeing Sabella beside him,

begged him to help. There was little Sabella could do. He could not move Lagurara's body, but in answer to his plea for water he crammed some snow into a handkerchief and held it to his mouth. After that he tried to make the radio work but it was completely dead; when he returned to the others, however, to keep up their morale he told them that he had spoken with Santiago.

Later, Canessa and Zerbino retraced Sabella's steps to the pilots' cabin. They tried to push the instrument panel off Lagurara, but it was impossible to move it even half an inch. His seat was also fixed immovably in position. All they were able to do was remove the cushion at the back and thereby relieve some of the pressure on his chest.

As they struggled in this futile attempt to free him, Lagurara said over and over again, "We passed Curicó, we passed Curicó." Then, seeing that nothing could be done, he asked the two boys to fetch the revolver which he kept in his bag. The bag was nowhere to be seen, nor would Canessa and Zerbino have given him the gun if they had found it, because, as Catholics, they could not condone suicide. They asked him instead if they could use the radio to bring help and set the dial as Lagurara instructed, but the transmitter was dead.

Lagurara continued to beg for his revolver and then asked for water. Canessa climbed out of the cockpit and brought in some snow which he fed into Lagurara's mouth, but the man's thirst was pathological and insatiable. He was bleeding through the nose, and Canessa knew that he would not live for long.

The two "doctors" made their way back over the seat cushions to the rear of the plane and returned to the dark, narrow tunnel of moaning, screaming humanity. Those who had been extracted from the wreckage lay out on the snow, as the few who were fit and strong worked desperately to drag out those seats they could pry loose and clear some space on the floor of the plane. But the daylight was fading. By six it was almost dark and the temperature had sunk far below freezing. It was clear that rescue would not come that day, and so the wounded were brought back into the plane and the thirty-two survivors prepared for the night.

Starting Time		Finishing Time	
Reading Time		Reading Rate	
Comprehension		Vocabulary	

Comprehension — Read the following questions and statements. For each one, put an *x* in the box before the option that contains the most complete or accurate answer. Check your answers in the Answer Key on page 108.

1. The survivors agreed that an early rescue would be possible if the
   ☐ a. heavy snow would let up.
   ☐ b. injured could be transported.
   ☐ c. supplies would hold out.
   ☐ d. plane's radio were working.

2. The high altitude made
   ☐ a. extended visibility impossible.
   ☐ b. the cold more bearable.
   ☐ c. the survivors more active.
   ☐ d. physical efforts exhausting.

3. When Canessa first examined Parrado, he thought Parrado
   ☐ a. needed water.
   ☐ b. hadn't seen the piece of steel in his stomach.
   ☐ c. was uninjured.
   ☐ d. was dead.

4. The purpose of the selection is to
   ☐ a. supply a factual account of a tragedy.
   ☐ b. discourage people from traveling by air.
   ☐ c. stress the importance of air safety.
   ☐ d. show how medical students react under stress.

5. The injured pilot kept repeating, "We passed Curicó, we passed Curicó," to
   ☐ a. warn the survivors of possible dangers.
   ☐ b. help Zerbino locate medical supplies.
   ☐ c. give the others an idea of their position.
   ☐ d. tell the survivors that help was near.

6. The medical students
   ☐ a. rose to the occasion.
   ☐ b. aggravated the situation.
   ☐ c. complained of the conditions.
   ☐ d. practiced medicine illegally.

7. The plane, crew, and passengers were most probably saved from total destruction because of the
   ☐ a. skill of the pilot.
   ☐ b. depth of the snow.
   ☐ c. condition of the plane.
   ☐ d. morale of the passengers.

8. Which of the following best describes the tone of the selection?
   ☐ a. morbid sentimentality
   ☐ b. frightening realism
   ☐ c. exaggerated suspense
   ☐ d. helpless despair

9. Canessa and Zerbino were
   ☐ a. sensitive to the suffering of others.
   ☐ b. glad for the chance to try out their skills.
   ☐ c. repulsed by the wounds of many of the passengers.
   ☐ d. preoccupied with thoughts of Carlos Valeta.

10. Which of the following passages intensifies the tone of the selection?
    ☐ a. ". . . but the transmitter was dead."
    ☐ b. "It was almost impossible to walk in the snow. . . ."
    ☐ c. "Because of the clouds the light was already somber. . . ."
    ☐ d. ". . . come and give me a hand with these seats."

Comprehension Skills

1. recalling specific facts	6. making a judgment
2. retaining concepts	7. making an inference
3. organizing facts	8. recognizing tone
4. understanding the main idea	9. understanding characters
5. drawing a conclusion	10. appreciation of literary forms

Study Skills, Part One — Following is a passage with blanks where words have been omitted. Next to the passage are groups of five words, one group for each blank. Complete the passage by selecting the correct word for each of the blanks.

Comprehension and Reading, II

Other aspects of reading comprehension follow word recognition. They are often grouped in the ___(1)___ of retention, organization, interpretation, and appreciation.

(1)   places   objects
     countries   families   areas

In retention, the reader is called upon to isolate details, to recall specifics, and to retain concepts. All of those skills are applied to ___(2)___ facts that have been read.

The reader is also expected to organize as he or she reads. Ways to organize are as follows:

1. Classifying. A good reader will arrange facts in groups while reading. In that way, facts that contribute to the comprehension of a concept are seen as a unit, ___(3)___ from those that deal with other concepts.

2. Establishing a Sequence. For true understanding of the author's ideas the reader must be aware of the order in which events take place. It is easier to understand a fact when it is seen as part of a related ___(4)___ . Think of each new fact as following the previous one and adding to the next.

3. Following Directions. Too many readers fail to follow directions, despite the important role they play in comprehension. Following directions is an organizing skill that requires the reader to arrange facts and to understand the steps he or she must follow. Readers often do not heed directions because they are unable to ___(5)___ facts properly, or they are unable to establish a correct sequence.

4. Seeing Relationships. An author puts forth ideas in an organized fashion, presenting ___(6)___ the concepts needed to understand other, more complex concepts that follow. The reader must grasp that relationship for true comprehension.

5. Generalizing. This skill requires the reader to arrive at general rules or theories derived from the specific ___(7)___ that the author has presented.

(2)   remembering   enjoying
       rejecting   scattering   discarding

(3)   resulting   copied
       separate   starting   borrowed

(4)   series   division
       unit   standard   chapter

(5)   understand   separate
       classify   estimate   appreciate

(6)   first   next
       finally   wisely   falsely

(7)   wishes   pictures
       patterns   facts   conclusions

Study Skills, Part Two—Read the study skills passage again, paying special attention to the lesson being taught. Then, without looking back at the passage, complete each sentence below by writing in the missing word or words. Check the Answer Key on page 108 for the answers to Study Skills, Part One, and Study Skills, Part Two.

1. The comprehension skill that enables the reader to recall specifics is

    called _____ .

2. Classifying is one way the reader can _____ facts.

3. To establish a sequence, the reader must be aware of the _____

    of events.

4. Following directions demands that the reader establish a

    _____ sequence.

5. When the reader arrives at a rule or theory from specific facts, he is

    _____ .

Alive, II

by Piers Paul Read

Vocabulary—The five words below are from the story you are about to read. Study the words and their meanings. Then complete the ten sentences that follow, using one of the five words to fill in the blank in each sentence. Mark your answer by writing the letter of the word on the line before the sentence. Check your answers in the Answer Key on page 108.

A. strident: harsh and grating

B. sustenance: nourishment

C. repugnant: offensive; disgusting

D. allayed: calmed; relieved

E. deter: prevent or discourage

_____ 1. Chocolate and wine provided meager _____ for the 27 survivors.

_____ 2. Javier and Liliana Methol did not try to _____ the others from doing what they felt they had to do.

_____ 3. To most people, the idea of eating human flesh is _____ .

_____ 4. The boys _____ their fears by telling themselves that God wanted them to use any possible means for survival.

_____ 5. The boys knew that the dead bodies could provide the _____ they needed.

_____ 6. None of the survivors launched into a _____ lecture about the sin of eating human flesh.

_____ 7. The deep snow did not _____ Canessa from going outside to look for dead bodies.

_____ 8. Although the act of eating human flesh was _____ to Canessa, he forced himself to do it.

_____ 9. Chilean politicians made _____ speeches on the radio.

_____ 10. Liliana Methol's concerns could not be _____ , and so she did not eat any slivers of flesh.

If they were to survive much longer, they would have to eat the bodies of those who had died.

They awoke on the morning of Sunday, October 22, to face their tenth day on the mountain. First to leave the plane were Marcelo Pérez and Roy Harley. Roy had found a transistor radio between two seats and by using a modest knowledge of electronics, acquired when helping a friend construct a hi-fi system, he had been able to make it work. It was difficult to receive signals in the deep cleft between the huge mountains, so Roy made an aerial with strands of wire from the plane's electric circuits. While he turned the dial, Marcelo held the aerial and moved it around. They picked up scraps of broadcasts from Chile but no news of the rescue effort. All that came over the radio waves were the strident voices of Chilean politicians embroiled in the strike by the middle classes against the socialist government of President Allende.

Few of the other boys came out into the snow. Starvation was taking its effect. They were becoming weaker and more listless. When they stood up they felt faint and found it difficult to keep their balance. They felt cold, even when the sun rose to warm them, and their skin started to grow wrinkled like that of old men.

Their food supplies were running out. The daily ration of a scrap of chocolate, a capful of wine, and a teaspoonful of jam or canned fish—eaten slowly to make it last—was more torture than sustenance for these healthy, athletic boys; yet the strong shared it with the weak, the healthy with the injured. It was clear to them all that they could not survive much longer. It was not so much that they were consumed with ravenous hunger as that they felt them-selves grow weaker each day, and no knowledge of medi-cine or nutrition was required to predict how it would end.

Their minds turned to other sources of food. It seemed impossible that there should be nothing whatsoever growing in the Andes, for even the meanest form of plant life might provide some nutrition. In the immediate vicinity of the plane there was only snow. The nearest soil was a hundred feet beneath them. The only ground exposed to sun and air was barren mountain rock on which they found nothing but brittle lichens. They scraped some of it off and mixed it into a paste with melted snow, but the taste was bitter and disgusting, and as food it was worthless. Except for lichens there was nothing. Some thought of the cushions, but even these were not stuffed with straw. Nylon and foam rubber would not help them.

For some days several of the boys had realized that if they were to survive they would have to eat the bodies of those who had died in the crash. It was a ghastly prospect. The corpses lay around the plane in the snow, preserved by the intense cold in the state in which they had died. While the thought of cutting flesh from those who had been their friends was deeply repugnant to them all, a lucid appreciation of their predicament led them to consider it.

Gradually the discus-sion spread as these boys cautiously mentioned it to their friends or to those they thought would be sympa-thetic. Finally, Canessa brought it out into the open. He argued forcefully that they were not going to be rescued; that they would have to escape themselves, but that nothing could be done without food; and that the only food was human flesh. He used his knowledge of medicine to describe, in his penetrating, high-pitched voice, how their bodies were using up their reserves. "Every time you move," he said, "you use up part of your own body. Soon we shall be so weak that we won't have the strength even to cut the meat that is lying there before our eyes."

Canessa did not argue just from expediency. He insisted that they had a moral duty to stay alive by any means at their disposal, and because Canessa was earnest about his religious belief, great weight was given to what he said by the more pious among the survivors.

"It is meat," he said. "That's all it is. The souls have left their bodies and are in heaven with God. All that is left here are the carcasses, which are no more human beings than the dead flesh of the cattle we eat at home."

The truth of what he said was incontestable.

A meeting was called inside the Fairchild, and for the first time all twenty-seven survivors discussed the issue which faced them—whether or not they should eat the bodies of the dead to survive. Canessa, Zerbino, Fernández, and Fito Strauch repeated the arguments they had used before. If they did not they would die. It was their moral obligation to live, for their own sake and for the sake of their families. God wanted them to live, and He had given them the means to do so in the dead bodies of their friends. If God had not wished them to live, they would have been killed in the accident; it would be wrong now to reject this gift of life because they were too squeamish.

"But what have we done," asked Marcelo, "that God now asks us to eat the bodies of our dead friends?"

There was a moment's hesistation. Then Zerbino turned to his captain and said, "But what do you think *they* would have thought?"

Marcelo did not answer.

"I know," Zerbino went on, "that if my dead body could help you to stay alive, then I'd certainly want you to use it. In fact, if I do die and you don't eat me, then I'll come back from wherever I am and give you a good kick in the ass."

This argument allayed many doubts, for however

reluctant each boy might be to eat the flesh of a friend, all of them agreed with Zerbino. There and then they made a pact that if any more of them were to die, their bodies were to be used as food.

Marcelo still shrank from a decision. He and his diminishing party of optimists held onto the hope of rescue, but few of the others any longer shared their faith. Indeed, a few of the younger boys went over to the pessimists—or the realists, as they considered themselves—with some resentment against Marcelo Pérez and Pancho Delgado. They felt they had been deceived. The rescue they had been promised had not come.

The latter were not without support, however. Coche Inciarte and Numa Turcatti, both strong, tough boys with an inner gentleness, told their companions that while they did not think it would be wrong, they knew that they themselves could not do it. Liliana Methol agreed with them. Her manner was calm as always but, like the others, she grappled with the emotions the issue aroused. Her instinct to survive was strong, her longing for her children was acute, but the thought of eating human flesh horrified her. She did not think it wrong; she could distinguish between sin and physical revulsion, and a social taboo was not a law of God. "But," she said, "as long as there is a chance of rescue, as long as there is *something* left to eat, even if it is only a morsel of chocolate, then I can't do it."

Javier Methol agreed with his wife but would not deter others from doing what they felt must be done. No one suggested that God might want them to choose to die. They all believed that virtue lay in survival and that eating their dead friends would in no way endanger their souls, but it was one thing to decide and another to act.

Their discussions had continued most of the day, and by midafternoon they knew that they must act now or not at all, yet they sat inside the plane in total silence. At last a group of four—Canessa, Maspons, Zerbino, and Fito Strauch—rose and went out into the snow. Few followed them. No one wished to know who was going to cut the meat or from which body it was to be taken.

Most of the bodies were covered by snow, but the buttocks of one protruded a few yards from the plane. With no exchange of words Canessa knelt, bared the skin, and cut into the flesh with a piece of broken glass. It was frozen hard and difficult to cut, but he persisted until he had cut away twenty slivers the size of matchsticks. He then stood up, went back to the plane, and placed them on the roof.

Inside there was silence. The boys cowered in the Fairchild. Canessa told them that the meat was there on the roof, drying in the sun, and that those who wished to do so should come out and eat it. No one came, and again Canessa took it upon himself to prove his resolution. He prayed to God to help him do what he knew to be right and then took a piece of meat in his hand. He hesitated. Even with his mind so firmly made up, the horror of the act paralyzed him. His hand would neither

rise to his mouth nor fall to his side while the revulsion which possessed him struggled with his stubborn will. The will prevailed. The hand rose and pushed the meat into his mouth. He swallowed it.

He felt triumphant. His conscience had overcome a primitive, irrational taboo. He was going to survive.

Later that evening, small groups of boys came out of the plane to follow his example. Zerbino took a strip and swallowed it as Canessa had done, but it stuck in his throat. He scooped a handful of snow into his mouth and managed to wash it down. Fito Strauch followed his example, then Maspons and Vizintin and others.

Meanwhile Gustavo Nicolich, the tall, curly-haired boy, only twenty years old, who had done so much to keep up the morale of his young friends, wrote to his *novia* in Montevido.

Most dear Rosina:

I am writing to you from inside the plane (our *petit hotel* for the moment). It is sunset and has started to be rather cold and windy which it usually does at this hour of the evening. Today the weather was wonderful—a beautiful sun and very hot. It reminded me of the days on the beach with you— the big difference being that then we would be going to have lunch at your place at midday whereas now I'm stuck outside the plane without any food at all.

Today, on top of everything else, it was rather depressing and a lot of the others began to get discouraged (today is the tenth day we have been here), but luckily this gloom did not spread to me because I get incredible strength just by thinking that I'm going to see you again. Another of the things leading to the general depression is that in a while the food will run out: we have only got two cans of seafood (small), one bottle of white wine, and a little cherry brandy left, which for twenty-six men (well, there are also boys who want to be men) is nothing.

One thing which will seem incredible to you— it seems unbelievable to me—is that today we started to cut up the dead in order to eat them. There is nothing else to do. I prayed to God from the bottom of my heart that this day would never come, but it has and we have to face it with courage and faith. Faith, because I came to the conclusion that the bodies are there because God put them there and since the only thing that matters is the soul, I don't have to feel great remorse; and if the day came and I could save someone with my body, I would gladly do it.

I don't know how you, Mama, Papa, or the children can be feeling; you don't know how sad it made me to think that you are suffering, and I constantly ask God to reassure you and give us courage because that is the only way of getting out of this. I think that soon there will be a happy ending for everyone.

You'll get a shock when you see me. I am dirty, with a beard, and a little thinner, with a big gash on my head, another one on my chest which has healed now, and one very small cut which I got today working in the cabin of the plane, besides various small cuts in the legs and on the shoulder; but in spite of it all, I'm all right.

Comprehension — Read the following questions and statements. For each one, put an *x* in the box before the option that contains the most complete or accurate answer. Check your answers in the Answer Key on page 108.

1. Liliana Methol could not bring herself to eat the bodies of the dead because she
   - ☐ a. could not disregard a social taboo.
   - ☐ b. was horrified by the thought of eating human flesh.
   - ☐ c. would not disobey God's law.
   - ☐ d. had lost interest in living.

2. Creeping starvation caused the athletes to
   - ☐ a. argue over food.
   - ☐ b. think unusual thoughts.
   - ☐ c. give up all hope.
   - ☐ d. submit to fate.

3. The boys decided to eat the flesh of their dead friends
   - ☐ a. as soon as they realized the nutritional value of such action.
   - ☐ b. only after hopes of a rescue faded.
   - ☐ c. after they ran out of all food supplies.
   - ☐ d. before realizing the consequences of their actions.

4. Another title for this selection could be
   - ☐ a. The Moment of Truth.
   - ☐ b. God's Children.
   - ☐ c. Survival of the Fittest.
   - ☐ d. The Great Unknown.

5. To the survivors, the strident voices of Chilean politicians must have seemed
   - ☐ a. like a ray of hope.
   - ☐ b. to be an answer to their prayers.
   - ☐ c. important and comforting.
   - ☐ d. unrealistic and futile.

6. The process by which the survivors decided to eat human flesh to save themselves was nothing less than
   - ☐ a. traumatic.   ☐ c. pointless.
   - ☐ b. ridiculous.   ☐ d. deceptive.

7. In a warmer climate, the dead bodies would have
   - ☐ a. started to decompose.
   - ☐ b. seemed more appetizing.
   - ☐ c. been impossible to cut up.
   - ☐ d. provided less nourishment.

8. The author's position concerning the personal decisions each survivor had to make is
   - ☐ a. critical.
   - ☐ b. unknown.
   - ☐ c. sentimental.
   - ☐ d. sympathetic.

9. Canessa was
   - ☐ a. indecisive.
   - ☐ b. irrational.
   - ☐ c. determined.
   - ☐ d. callous.

10. The author tries to make the reader
   - ☐ a. believe that eating human flesh is a natural act.
   - ☐ b. despise the boys who ate their dead friends.
   - ☐ c. understand why the boys acted as they did.
   - ☐ d. realize that survival is more important than moral beliefs.

Comprehension Skills

1. recalling specific facts	6. making a judgment
2. retaining concepts	7. making an inference
3. organizing facts	8. recognizing tone
4. understanding the main idea	9. understanding characters
5. drawing a conclusion	10. appreciation of literary forms

Study Skills, Part One—Following is a passage with blanks where words have been omitted. Next to the passage are groups of five words, one group for each blank. Complete the passage by selecting the correct word for each of the blanks.

Comprehension and Reading, III

As we have seen, retention and organization are two aspects of comprehension that are expected of the reader. Two other such areas are interpretation and appreciation. They are made up of the following six skills:

1. Understanding the Main Idea. As you would expect, proper interpretation of the material is based on understanding the main idea. Very often, though, the main idea is not ___(1)___ but must be gathered or interpreted by the reader.

(1) found   appreciated   hinted   understood   stated

2. Drawing Conclusions. Based on the ideas presented, the reader must make the only judgment or form the only ___(2)___ allowed by the facts. There should be no doubt about which conclusion the author expects you to reach.

(2) opinion   principle   index   illustration   graph

3. Making Inferences. Unlike a conclusion, an inference is a reasonable judgment based on the facts. The idea you infer may not be the only one suggested, but it will clearly be the one the author ___(3)___ . Making inferences is one of the most critical areas of comprehension demanded of the reader.

(3) discarded   denied   intended   interrupted   interposed

4. Predicting Outcomes. Authors use ideas to ___(4)___ the reader to certain ends or objectives. The outcome may not be disclosed outright, but authors also provide a groundwork of the facts you need to predict the intended ___(5)___ .

(4) lead   lend   discourage   follow   divert

5. Making a Judgment. Sometimes the author expects readers to make a judgment suggested by the facts and arguments.

(5) collapse   result   success   behavior   record

6. Recognizing Tone. Finally, we are expected to demonstrate a sensitive appreciation and ___(6)___ of the author's work. We do that by recognizing tone—reacting to the joy or sadness of the article. We also understand and identify with characters. Finally, we visualize the realness the author has strived to ___(7)___ , and we see humor— and are moved to laughter—when that has been the goal.

(6) dislike   criticism   awareness   fear   hatred

(7) destroy   create   imitate   overcome   employ

Study Skills, Part Two—Read the study skills passage again, paying special attention to the lesson being taught. Then, without looking back at the passage, complete each sentence below by writing in the missing word or words. Check the Answer Key on page 108 for the answers to Study Skills, Part One, and Study Skills, Part Two.

1. Interpretation requires the most use of _____ from the reader.

2. The facts presented by the author allow only one _____ to be reached.

3. The idea you infer may not be the only one _____ .

4. The author lays a groundwork of facts from which the reader can _____ the outcome.

5. Reacting to the joy or sadness of a story is recognizing _____ .

Answer Key

Selection 1

Vocabulary

1. B	6. B
2. C	7. E
3. E	8. A
4. A	9. D
5. D	10. C

Comprehension

1. b	6. b
2. a	7. b
3. d	8. a
4. c	9. c
5. c	10. d

Study Skills, Part One

1. question	6. supporting
2. important	7. field
3. approach	
4. plan	
5. places	

Study Skills, Part Two

1. Preview
2. scout
3. picture
4. examples
5. organize

Selection 2

Vocabulary

1. B	6. E
2. C	7. A
3. C	8. E
4. D	9. D
5. B	10. A

Comprehension

1. a	6. a
2. b	7. b
3. b	8. a
4. b	9. c
5. d	10. a

Study Skills, Part One

1. aware	6. interest
2. arguments	7. content
3. information	
4. humor	
5. shock	

Study Skills, Part Two

1. reading the titles
2. feelings
3. titles
4. digest
5. words

Selection 3

Vocabulary

1. A	6. A
2. D	7. C
3. C	8. E
4. D	9. E
5. B	10. B

Comprehension

1. a	6. c
2. b	7. a
3. c	8. b
4. c	9. b
5. d	10. b

Study Skills, Part One

1. reader	6. learn
2. written	7. facets
3. set	
4. end	
5. author	

Study Skills, Part Two

1. introduction
2. setting
3. important
4. summarize
5. skim

Selection 4

Vocabulary

1. B	6. D
2. C	7. E
3. A	8. C
4. D	9. A
5. B	10. E

Comprehension

1. a	6. d
2. c	7. c
3. b	8. a
4. a	9. d
5. d	10. a

Study Skills, Part One

1. inquiring	6. expects
2. activity	7. create
3. prereading	
4. outline	
5. technique	

Study Skills, Part Two

1. ask questions
2. learn
3. presentation
4. contrast
5. following

Selection 5

Vocabulary

1. C	6. C
2. A	7. D
3. D	8. B
4. B	9. E
5. E	10. A

Comprehension

1. b	6. a
2. b	7. b
3. a	8. c
4. d	9. b
5. c	10. a

Study Skills, Part One

1. time	6. works
2. interfering	7. best
3. really	
4. quiz	
5. enough	

Study Skills, Part Two

1. problems
2. attention
3. Motivation
4. goal
5. distractions

Selection 6

Vocabulary

1. C	6. A
2. D	7. B
3. B	8. A
4. E	9. D
5. C	10. E

Comprehension

1. a	6. a
2. c	7. c
3. c	8. a
4. d	9. c
5. c	10. b

Study Skills, Part One

1. finishes	6. unfinished
2. challenge	7. related
3. clock	
4. periods	
5. complete	

Study Skills, Part Two

1. time
2. shorter
3. spread
4. tasks
5. list

Selection 7

Vocabulary

1. D	6. C
2. B	7. E
3. E	8. B
4. C	9. A
5. A	10. D

Comprehension

1. b	6. d
2. d	7. a
3. d	8. a
4. c	9. b
5. a	10. c

Study Skills, Part One

1. employ	6. facts
2. introduced	7. minimize
3. want	
4. entire	
5. questions	

Study Skills, Part Two

1. plan
2. tried
3. review
4. previewing
5. Generalize

Selection 8

Vocabulary

1. A	6. B
2. E	7. E
3. D	8. D
4. A	9. B
5. C	10. C

Comprehension

1. c	6. b
2. a	7. c
3. c	8. a
4. a	9. b
5. b	10. b

Study Skills, Part One

1. reader	6. places
2. introduced	7. important
3. appear	
4. value	
5. aware	

Study Skills, Part Two

1. obvious
2. letters
3. 4
4. beginning
5. summaries

Selection 9

Vocabulary

1. E	6. C
2. D	7. D
3. C	8. A
4. A	9. E
5. B	10. B

Comprehension

1. d	6. d
2. c	7. a
3. b	8. a
4. d	9. a
5. c	10. a

Study Skills, Part One

1. advance	6. identify
2. equal	7. alert
3. opposing	
4. previous	
5. similar	

Study Skills, Part Two

1. guide
2. difficult
3. forward
4. series
5. stronger

Selection 10

Vocabulary

1. A	6. A
2. D	7. C
3. E	8. D
4. B	9. B
5. E	10. C

Comprehension

1. a	6. c
2. b	7. d
3. a	8. a
4. a	9. d
5. c	10. d

Study Skills, Part One

1. urge	6. identify
2. job	7. statements
3. result	
4. pause	
5. meaning	

Study Skills, Part Two

1. new
2. specific
3. finished
4. textbooks
5. beginning

Selection 11

Vocabulary

1. C	6. E
2. A	7. B
3. C	8. A
4. B	9. E
5. D	10. D

Comprehension

1. b	6. d
2. a	7. b
3. a	8. c
4. c	9. b
5. a	10. d

Study Skills, Part One

1. important	6. intends
2. concluding	7. major
3. draw	
4. distinction	
5. subject	

Study Skills, Part Two

1. Terminal
2. end
3. new
4. finality
5. subject

Selection 12

Vocabulary

1. E	6. D
2. A	7. A
3. C	8. C
4. B	9. B
5. E	10. D

Comprehension

1. b	6. a
2. a	7. a
3. d	8. c
4. d	9. a
5. b	10. c

Study Skills, Part One

1. continuing	6. forward
2. direction	7. turn
3. different	
4. said	
5. significance	

Study Skills, Part Two

1. Counter
2. turnabout
3. lead
4. meaning
5. prepare

Selection 13

Vocabulary

1. C	6. A
2. E	7. E
3. B	8. B
4. A	9. C
5. D	10. D

Comprehension

1. a	6. a
2. c	7. c
3. c	8. b
4. a	9. a
5. b	10. b

Study Skills, Part One

1. well	6. opening
2. constructed	7. information
3. subject	
4. background	
5. reason	

Study Skills, Part Two

1. use
2. well organized
3. learn
4. practical
5. preface/introduction

Selection 14

Vocabulary
1. C	6. A
2. E	7. D
3. D	8. A
4. B	9. E
5. C	10. B

Comprehension
1. b	6. d
2. a	7. b
3. c	8. b
4. a	9. d
5. c	10. a

Study Skills, Part One
1. text	6. current
2. early	7. additional
3. presented	
4. background	
5. reference	

Study Skills, Part Two
1. organized
2. Historical
3. complex
4. preread
5. information

Selection 15

Vocabulary
1. B	6. E
2. E	7. D
3. C	8. C
4. D	9. A
5. A	10. B

Comprehension
1. c	6. b
2. b	7. b
3. b	8. b
4. b	9. b
5. d	10. b

Study Skills, Part One
1. name	6. powerless
2. topics	7. easier
3. evaluate	
4. checks	
5. opposite	

Study Skills, Part Two
1. subject
2. alphabetical
3. number
4. familiar
5. supplement

Selection 16

Vocabulary
1. B	6. A
2. E	7. E
3. C	8. D
4. D	9. C
5. B	10. A

Comprehension
1. c	6. c
2. b	7. c
3. a	8. d
4. c	9. b
5. b	10. b

Study Skills, Part One
1. wise	6. parting
2. limits	7. main
3. clue	
4. visual	
5. expected	

Study Skills, Part Two
1. organization
2. subheads
3. false
4. closing
5. skim

Selection 17

Vocabulary
1. E	6. D
2. A	7. C
3. B	8. B
4. C	9. E
5. A	10. D

Comprehension
1. c	6. b
2. c	7. c
3. a	8. a
4. d	9. b
5. b	10. a

Study Skills, Part One
1. own	6. pages
2. worthy	7. understand
3. unmarked	
4. mark	
5. important	

Study Skills, Part Two
1. creative
2. frequently
3. Brackets
4. number
5. abbreviations

Selection 18

Vocabulary
1. C	6. B
2. A	7. E
3. B	8. D
4. D	9. E
5. C	10. A

Comprehension
1. c	6. c
2. b	7. c
3. c	8. b
4. c	9. a
5. a	10. d

Study Skills, Part One
1. moving	6. parts
2. word	7. method
3. memorizing	
4. unfamiliar	
5. listening	

Study Skills, Part Two
1. mental
2. sight
3. recognize
4. phonics
5. analysis

Selection 19

Vocabulary
1. A	6. D
2. D	7. B
3. E	8. E
4. C	9. B
5. A	10. C

Comprehension
1. d	6. a
2. d	7. b
3. d	8. b
4. a	9. a
5. c	10. a

Study Skills, Part One
1. areas	6. first
2. remembering	7. facts
3. separate	
4. series	
5. classify	

Study Skills, Part Two
1. retention
2. organize
3. order
4. correct
5. generalizing

Selection 20

Vocabulary
1. B	6. A
2. E	7. E
3. C	8. C
4. D	9. A
5. B	10. D

Comprehension
1. b	6. a
2. b	7. a
3. b	8. d
4. a	9. c
5. d	10. c

Study Skills, Part One
1. stated	6. awareness
2. opinion	7. create
3. intended	
4. lead	
5. result	

Study Skills, Part Two
1. judgment
2. conclusion
3. suggested
4. predict
5. tone

Bibliography

Every effort has been made to locate the author, publisher, place of publication, and copyright date for each selection.

Allen, William. "A Whole Society of Loners and Dreamers." In *Saturday Review.* New York: Saturday Review, 1972.

Bach, Richard. *Jonathan Livingston Seagull.* New York: Macmillan Publishing Company, 1970.

Caldwell, Erskine. "Warm River." In *We Are the Living.* Boston: Little, Brown and Company, Inc., 1933.

Corlander, Harold, and George Herzog. "The Cow-Tail Switch." In *The Cow-Tail Switch and Other Stories.* Orlando, Florida: Holt, Rinehart & Winston, Inc. 1962.

Gorman, James. "Bat Guano Can Make a Man Come Face-to-Face with His Values." In *Discover* magazine. New York: Family Media, 1987.

————. "Will the Weather Channel Save America?" In *Discover* magazine. New York: Family Media, 1987.

Hersch, Patricia. "Coming of Age on City Streets." In *Psychology Today.* Washington, DC: American Psychological Association, 1988.

Honan, William H. "The Grand Canyon by Chopper." In *Saturday Review/Science.* New York: Saturday Review, 1973.

Jensen, Pauline L. "Henrietta, an Intelligent Fish." In *The National Humane Review.* Denver: American Humane Association, 1973.

Klass, Sheila Solomon. "A Transcendent Moment." In *Ms.* magazine. New York: Ms. Magazine Corporation, 1988.

Leacock, Stephen. "How We Kept Mother's Day." In *Laugh with Leacock.* New York: Dodd, Mead & Company, Inc., 1958.

Osada, Dr. Arata. *Children of the A-Bomb.* New York: G. P. Putnam's Sons, 1959.

Petersen, Robert. "Why Not Bicycle to Work?" In *Bicycling.* Emmaus, Pennsylvania: Rodale Press, 1968.

Rapoport, Roger. "The Science of Being Santa." In *Saturday Review/Science.* New York: Saturday Review, 1973.

Read, Piers Paul. *Alive: The Story of the Andes Survivors.* Philadelphia: J. B. Lippincott Company, 1974.

Revkin, Andrew C. "Organ Hunter." In *Discover* magazine. New York: Family Media, 1988.

Yoshiki, Hayama. "Letter Found in a Cement Barrel." In *Modern Japanese Stories.* Edited and translated by Ivan Morris. Rutland, Vermont: Charles E. Tuttle Co. Inc., 1961.

Words per Minute

Selection No. of Words	1	2	3	4	5	6	7	8	9	10	11	12	13	14	15	16	17	18	19	20
(No. of Words)	1585	1515	1335	2050	1405	1580	1870	2165	1820	1760	1760	1620	1700	1700	1985	1670	1710	1895	2380	2220
1:20	1220	1140	1005	1540	1055	1190	1410	1630	1400	1325	1325	1220	1280	1280	1525	1255	1290	1425	1790	1670
1:40	990	915	805	1235	845	950	1130	1305	1140	1060	1060	975	1025	1025	1240	1005	1035	1140	1435	1340
2:00	790	760	670	1025	705	790	940	1085	910	880	880	810	850	850	990	835	860	950	1190	1110
2:20	690	650	575	880	605	680	805	930	790	755	755	695	730	730	865	715	735	815	1020	955
2:40	610	570	500	770	530	595	705	815	700	660	660	610	640	640	765	630	645	710	895	835
3:00	560	505	445	685	470	525	625	720	605	585	585	540	565	565	660	555	570	630	795	740
3:20	510	455	400	615	420	475	565	650	550	530	530	485	510	510	600	500	515	570	715	665
3:40	440	415	365	560	385	430	510	590	505	480	480	445	465	465	550	455	470	520	650	605
4:00	395	380	335	515	350	395	470	540	450	440	440	405	425	425	495	420	430	475	595	555
4:20	370	350	310	475	325	365	435	500	420	405	405	375	395	395	465	385	395	440	550	515
4:40	345	325	285	440	300	340	400	465	390	380	380	350	365	365	430	360	370	405	510	475
5:00	315	305	265	410	280	315	375	435	360	350	350	325	340	340	395	335	345	380	475	445
5:20	300	285	250	385	265	295	350	405	340	330	330	305	320	320	370	315	320	355	445	415
5:40	285	270	235	360	250	280	330	385	320	310	310	285	300	300	355	295	305	335	420	390
6:00	265	255	225	340	235	265	315	360	300	295	295	270	285	285	335	280	285	315	395	370
6:20	250	240	210	325	220	250	295	340	285	280	280	255	270	270	315	265	270	300	375	350
6:40	240	230	200	310	210	235	280	325	270	265	265	245	255	255	300	250	260	285	360	335
7:00	225	215	190	295	200	225	270	310	255	250	250	230	245	245	280	240	245	270	340	315
7:20	215	205	180	280	190	215	255	295	245	240	240	220	230	230	270	230	235	260	325	305
7:40	210	200	175	270	185	205	245	285	235	230	230	210	220	220	260	220	225	250	310	290
8:00	200	190	165	255	175	200	235	270	225	220	220	205	215	215	245	210	215	235	300	280
8:20	190	180	160	245	170	190	225	260	215	210	210	195	205	205	240	200	205	225	285	265
8:40	185	175	155	235	160	180	215	250	205	205	205	185	195	195	230	195	200	220	275	255
9:00	175	170	150	230	155	175	210	240	200	195	195	180	190	190	220	185	190	210	265	245
9:20	170	165	145	220	150	170	200	230	190	190	190	175	180	180	210	180	185	205	255	240
9:40	165	155	140	210	145	165	195	225	185	180	180	170	175	175	205	175	180	195	245	230
10:00	160	150	135	205	140	160	190	215	180	175	175	160	170	170	195	165	170	190	240	220
10:20	155	145	130	200	135	155	180	210	170	170	170	155	165	165	190	160	165	185	230	215
10:40	150	140	125	190	130	150	175	205	165	165	165	150	160	160	185	155	160	180	125	210
11:00	145	140	120	185	125	145	165	195	165	160	160	145	155	155	180	150	155	170	215	205
11:20	140	135	120	180	120	140	160	190	160	155	155	145	150	150	175	150	150	165	210	200
11:40	135	130	115	175	115	135	155	185	155	150	150	140	145	145	170	145	145	165	205	195
12:00	130	125	110	170	115	130	150	180	150	145	145	135	140	140	165	140	145	160	200	190
12:20	130	125	120	165	110	130	150	175	145	140	140	130	140	140	160	135	140	155	195	185
12:40	125	120	115	160	105	125	145	170	140	135	135	130	135	135	155	130	135	150	190	180
13:00	120	115	110	160	105	120	140	165	135	130	130	125	130	130	150	130	130	145	185	175
13:20	120	115	110	155	105	120	135	160	130	130	130	120	130	130	150	125	130	140	180	170
13:40	115	110	100	150	100	115	135	160	130	125	125	120	125	125	145	120	125	140	175	165
14:00	115	110	100	145	100	115	130	155	125	125	125	115	120	120	140	120	125	135	170	165
14:20	110	105	95	145	95	110	130	150	125	120	125	115	120	120	140	115	120	130	165	160
14:40	110	105	90	140	95	110	130	150	125	120	120	110	115	115	135	115	115	130	160	155
15:00	105	100	90	135	95	105	125	145	120	120	120	110	115	115	130	110	115	125	160	150

Minutes and Seconds Elapsed

Progress Graph

Scores

Selection	Words per Minute	100	90	80	70	60	50	40	30	20
1										
2										
3										
4										
5										
6										
7										
8										
9										
10										
11										
12										
13										
14										
15										
16										
17										
18										
19										
20										

Comprehension Skills Profile

The graph below is designed to help you see your areas of comprehension weakness. Because all the comprehension questions in this text are coded, it is possible for you to determine which kinds of questions give you the most trouble.

On the graph below, keep a record of questions you have answered incorrectly. Following each selection, darken a square on the graph next to the number of the question missed. The columns are labeled with the selection numbers.

By looking at the chart and noting the number of shaded squares, you should be able to tell which areas of comprehension you are weak in. A large number of shaded squares across from a particular skill signifies an area of reading comprehension weakness. When you discover a particular weakness, give greater attention and time to answering questions of that type.

Further, you might wish to check with your instructor for recommendations of appropriate practice materials.

Categories of Comprehension Skills	Selection																			
	1	2	3	4	5	6	7	8	9	10	11	12	13	14	15	16	17	18	19	20
1. Recalling Specific Facts																				
2. Retaining Concepts																				
3. Organizing Facts																				
4. Understanding the Main Idea																				
5. Drawing a Conclusion																				
6. Making a Judgment																				
7. Making an Inference																				
8. Recognizing Tone																				
9. Understanding Characters																				
10. Appreciation of Literary Forms																				